Extreme MAKEOVER
HOME EDITION ™

THE OFFICIAL COMPANION BOOK

FIRST EDITION

ISBN: 1-4013-0819-8

Hyperion books are available for special promotions and premiums.
For details contact Michael Rentas, Assistant Director, Inventory Operations, Hyperion, 77 West 66th Street, 11th Floor, New York, New York 10023, or call 212-456-0133.

10 9 8 7 6 5 4 3 2 1

Special thanks to:

Bob Miller, President, Hyperion
Ellen Archer, Senior Vice President & Publisher, Hyperion
Will Schwalbe, Senior Vice President & Editor-in-Chief, Hyperion
Gretchen Young, Executive Editor, Hyperion
Zareen Jaffery, Associate Editor, Hyperion
Linda Prather, Director of Preproduction/Production, Hyperion
Deirdre Smerillo, Contracts Director, Hyperion
Bruce Gersh, Senior Vice President, Business Development, ABC Entertainment
Melissa Harling, Manager, Business Development, ABC Entertainment
Vicki Dummer, Vice President Alternative Series and Specials, ABC Entertainment
Tracey Myman, ABC Legal Counsel
Dan Richards, Vice President, ABC Photography
Jason Hoffman, Director, ABC Photography
Tom Forman, Executive Producer, *EM:HE*
Julie Link, Development Producer, Endemol
Lisa Higgins, SVP of Production, Endemol

Extreme Makeover: Home Edition — The Official Companion Book
was produced for Hyperion by Madison Press Books:

Jonathan Schmidt and **Carolyn Jackson,** Project Editors
Shima Aoki, Assistant Editor
Jim Hynes and **Rob Lutes,** Writers
Costa Leclerc Design, Book and Cover Design
Christopher Jackson, Director, Business Development

Thanks to **Ari Woog** for photographs that appear on the following pages:
4, 5, 74, 78, 79, 92-93, 95, 97, 98, 99, 110, 111, 118-119, 138-139, 152, 158-159, and 176.

Cover photography provided by **ABC, Inc.**

Contents

Tom Forman, Executive Producer
What Were We Thinking?

By the time Ty takes up the bullhorn outside a family's home, weeks of work by behind-the-scenes staff have already gone into the episode.

Executive Producer Tom Forman remembers that they used to promise neighbors that noisy work would be done during the day. "It became clear, real fast, that wouldn't work," he jokes. "But people have been incredible. We keep them up all night and they make coffee for the workers. I've never seen anything like it."

It's been two seasons. More than 30 episodes. Skyrocketing ratings, millions of weekly viewers, a rash of awards, including the 2004 Family Television Award for Best Reality Show and the 2005 People's Choice Award for Favorite Reality Show (Makeover) and an Emmy nomination for Outstanding Reality Program.

Could anyone have imagined such a crazy idea would be such a success?

"Never in a million years," admits *Extreme Makeover: Home Edition* Executive Producer Tom Forman. "It's been unbelievable. An absolutely incredible ride."

What's the key to the show's exhilarating climb to the top?

Simple, says Forman. "People love a happy ending. Every one of us has gone through hard times. And every one of us can identify with the families on the show." But it's more than that. "Traveling around the country doing these makeovers, I think we've seen that we live in a world where neighbors aren't really neighbors anymore. They're people you've never met living in a house you've never been in. And I don't think they like it. This show," Forman explains, "connects people with their community. They see us making a difference in the life of a family, and it inspires them to do the same.

"Sometimes that means they come down, grab a paintbrush, and help us finish the house. Sometimes they start their own projects in their own communities for people who desperately need the help." Maybe not on the same scale as the show, continues Forman, "but in many ways, those personal projects are even cooler and more important than what we do on TV. They're real people making a real difference."

He says the show has received hundreds of letters from surprised and grateful families who have been helped out by friends and neighbors. "They are planting gardens, mending fences, weeding overgrown gardens, and cleaning vacant lots. This is so much more than a television show. It's about a community coming together to help out one of their own. It begins with us. But it doesn't end with us. Folks are coming together and working together and realizing that they can make a difference. It's an incredibly rewarding thing to see."

For all its rewards, Forman concedes it has also been the most demanding show he has ever been associated with.

"It combines two of scariest things imaginable," he jokes, "home construction and putting on a weekly television show. And we do it simultaneously!"

The shooting schedule is grueling. "My staff signed up to work on a pilot—just one episode for ABC to take a look at. It was supposed to be a five-week gig. Well, they've been here ever since. Two crazy years. And we never stop. Ever."

It takes the incredible dedication and hard work of nearly 2,000 people each week to get the show on the air, plus the patience, goodwill, and generosity of the hundreds of neighbors who smile through a literal invasion by the huge production and construction crew.

"We generally shut down seven square blocks of a neighborhood. We divert traffic, make noise, and set up lights everywhere. But folks still treat us like family. Early on we used to promise that all the noisy work would be done during the day and nighttime hours would be restricted to quiet work, like painting." Forman laughs at the memory. "Well, it became clear real fast that wouldn't work. It's three in the morning and it's time to fire up the giant diesel excavator. What can you do? But people have been incredible. We keep them up all night—and they make coffee for the workers! I've never seen anything like it."

With all the success, how has the show changed?

"When we showed up in a neighborhood," says Forman, "we used to joke that we had to set up a small city. Now it's no joke: it's a big city.

"This is not a show about egos," Forman concludes. "This is not about product placement. It's not about shiny appliances or big houses or being on TV. It's not about ratings or awards. This is all about community. It's about making a difference in the life of a good family that's down on its luck and just needs a helping hand. We all need a little help sometime.

"It's been an incredible ride. And it's not over. Not by a long shot!"

There's not a lot of time, but every break provides an occasion to ham it up. Some 2,000 people are involved in getting the show on the air each week.

Demolition is often the only way to go. Ready, set...bye-bye old house!

GOOOOO MORNING! MORNING!

Ty

Paige

Paul

Constance

Michael

Tracy

Ed

Eduardo

Preston

Powers FAMILY

The Powers family of Santa Clarita, California, knew what they were getting into when they purchased their 1960s-era ranch-style house. It was a fixer-upper, and parents Rodney and Kristin Powers had lots of ideas and plans for getting it into shape.

Those plans were cruelly dashed when they learned that their youngest daughter, Olivia, was diagnosed with a life-threatening form of acute lymphacetic leukemia at the tender age of 3.

The Powers put their home improvement plans aside as they focused all of their energies on Olivia. Her difficult and often painful treatment took almost three long years. Olivia, now 6, is finally healthy again, and the Powers are ready to think about giving the family home the attention it requires.

"This family really deserves it," says Ty as the Team bus rolls toward the Powers' home. "They don't need it, they deserve it."

The Design Team of Ty, Michael, Paul, Constance, Tracy, and Preston—bounds down the bus steps as it rolls to a stop in front of the Powers' home.

Ty, bullhorn in hand, prepares to surprise the family with a unique wake-up call. "Good Morning Powers family!"

Rodney, Kristin, daughter Brittni, 14, son Reid, 11, and a beaming Olivia are barely over the shock of seeing Ty and the designers on their doorstep when they hear more incredible news. While their home is being renovated, they'll be vacationing at the gorgeous Atlantis Paradise Island resort in the Bahamas.

"I've never been on vacation," Kristin says.

Kristin Powers is shocked to learn—via Ty's bullhorn announcement—that her family has been chosen for an *Extreme Makeover: Home Edition* renovation.

THE HOUSE

As the Powers lead the Team on a tour of the house, it becomes clear that it needs an update—badly.

The living room is small and crowded; the kitchen is outdated; one bathroom is under repair; and the entire house needs a fresh coat of paint. A huge brown arch dominates the front of the house.

"The arch has got to go," Preston quickly decides. "It's not cool."

In the cluttered garage, Rodney proudly shows Ty his beloved pickup truck, which is filled with an astounding collection of junk. Stepping gingerly into the backyard, the Team conducts a quick survey and concedes the yard, at least, is not bad. It even has an in-ground swimming pool.

"We'd love a slide," suggests Kristin.

One thing the Design Team learns it will not be changing is a wall panel in the den. Hand-stenciled by Kristin when Olivia was going through the worst and most painful period of her

BIRTH OF THE BULLHORN!!!!

"We gave Ty the megaphone because we worried maybe his voice wasn't loud enough to wake the family. We just grabbed a megaphone from an assistant and shoved it into his hands and said, 'Here!'"

—*Executive Producer Tom Forman*

cancer treatment, the message became a motto for the family during a very trying time.

"Take one day at a time...live, love & laugh...be strong, be you... breathe," the mural proclaims.

"It kept us going every day," explains Kristin.

Ty ushers the Powers off on their vacation, and the Team sits down for the first time to start planning the renovation. With time at a premium, they settle quickly on a Craftsman-style design featuring and an open-concept interior to create more space—a lot more space.

After much back-and-forth discussion, the Team decides it is ready to begin. There is just one more small detail to take care of first.

Ty calls the Powers family in their limo. He asks little Olivia about her room. He has decided to take on the renovation of her space as his "special project."

Next, Ty nominates a somewhat doubtful Constance to oversee the construction of one of the renovation's centerpieces—a giant pirate ship, complete with slide for the pool!

More than 50 workers under the supervision of burly contractor Pat Shinn and his identical twin brother, Mike, swarm the house.

The demolition begins.

"Wow, man! This is Ben Hur, baby! I've never seen anything like it!" Ty enthuses.

Not so fast, Ty! Pat has estimated that the job is basically a four-month remodel. Ty grins and shakes his head. Pat turns back to his workers.

"You got seven days—168 hours—to get it done," Pat informs the crew. "You guys up to the task?" A huge cheer goes up. There are no doubters in this group. It's pedal to the metal.

"You look at Pat, and Pat gives you hope," says Paul.

Tracy and Michael team up to design the interior and handle furnishings. Paul takes on a myriad of projects, while Ty heads to Olivia's room. Meanwhile, it's up to Constance to oversee just about everything else—including the pirate ship.

Free-spirited Preston, meanwhile, manages to rattle almost everyone with his lack of planning and off-the-cuff methods. The contractors are doubtful and Constance, in particular, is worried that he has not provided her with any detailed plans or blueprints.

"We only finished hiring the Design Team 14 hours before the shoot began. So when the family runs out and Ty introduces the Team for the first time, he has no idea, really, who they are! Watching that episode is like watching a time capsule."

—Tom Forman

Executive Producer Tom Forman recalls the thoughts running through his head the first time they watched a crew tear into a house. "What have we done?" He laughs. "I hope we can put this thing back up, because literally we didn't know. We had no idea! It was the episode where we made up everything."

Like any good team, the members resolve their differences. Ty decides to take a break and have some fun with the family on a conference call "update." With hammers pounding and saws buzzing in the background, he fools them into thinking they've picked pink shag carpeting for their new "dream-come-true" living room.

The house is going up fast. The pirate ship, however, has hit stormy seas and is behind schedule. The Team cannot come to a decision about the design. Meanwhile, the clock keeps ticking and the yard is just a pile of dirt.

With less than 24 hours to go, everyone is exhausted.

"I just hope this is all worth it," Paul says.

WELCOME TO YOUR NEW HOME!

When the limousine turns the corner, the Powers are overwhelmed by the welcome they receive. Hundreds of neighbors and well-wishers have turned out for the "unveiling." They pile out of the limo to enter their new home. Brittni's room has been transformed into combination surfer theme/tiki room complete with bamboo walls, surfboards, and a kitschy-cool hula lamp.

In Reid's room, Paul shows off the bed made from the back half of Rodney's pickup. As Rodney contemplates the loss of his beloved truck, the family moves to the garage. Not wanting to destroy any of the Powers' precious memories, Paul preserved the cab in the wacky drive-in/home theater he has made in the garage. In the backyard, the nearly 100 workers who transformed the home greet the incredulous family from the deck of the impressive pirate ship.

It's hard to believe there is more to come, but Ty has yet to reveal his special treat. He introduces Olivia to her new giant dollhouse bedroom.

"I could tell she really loved the room," recalls Ty. "To me that's the most important thing for this whole family and the whole story they went through. It's a great feeling to do this for these people."

Woslum FAMILY

Trent and Dawna Woslum lived in a mobile home for 10 years before buying their first home in Palmdale, California, a fixer-upper they purchased as a Christmas present for their three sons in December 2002. The house needed a lot of love and attention, and the Woslums had substantial renovation plans for it. But the family hadn't finished settling in when Trent, a sergeant in the California National Guard, was called up to serve in Iraq on Valentine's Day 2003.

With Trent overseas, Dawna had to return to work on top of caring for Steven, 12, Nicholas, 7, and Alex, 5, on her own. Between work, school, and shuttling the baseball-mad boys between Little League games and practices, there were not enough hours in the day for the exhausted mom to finish unpacking, let alone work on the house.

THE HOUSE

Shortly after dawn, Ty, Tracy, Constance, Paul, Michael, and Preston arrive to surprise the Woslums.

Their first impressions are favorable. From the exterior, the house is quite nice. But after a short tour of the inside, it quickly becomes clear to the Team that a lot of work will be needed to make this house a home. The rooms are sparsely furnished, small, and cramped, and the decorating is dull, dominated by whites and grays.

"We're at 32.3 hours from having them pull up to the front porch. We've got about 75 hours worth of work. You do the math."
—Michael

After a frantic final 24 hours the renovation is in "ship" shape—to the delight of the happy Powers clan.

fabulo-meter

Every room is going to have something that says, '**WOW**.'
—Michael

The family's dining room set consists of a folding table and four white plastic garden chairs.

"Weatherproof?" wonders Ty aloud.

"No," corrects Dawna, "spill-proof."

It gets worse, as the Team quickly discovers. The kitchen is outdated, with a gold plastic suspended ceiling. Nicholas and Alex share a tiny room. The family dog has destroyed the linoleum floor in the master bathroom, and the backyard, where the boys like to take batting practice, is narrow and overgrown in places. In the spacious garage, Ty finds a vanity Dawna inherited from her grandmother.

"It's really old, and it needs a lift, too," says Dawna.

THE RENOVATION BEGINS NOW!

There's no time to lose. After wishing the family bon voyage on a dream vacation to Disneyland, the Team gets down to business.

Inspired by its adobe tile roof, the Team chooses a Spanish hacienda style for the house and landscape.

"Color, color, color," says Michael. "There's going to be red, there's going to be terra cotta, there's going to be mustard. Every room is going to have something that says 'Wow.'"

The house needs more room. It will be a lot of work. But Ty has recruited a very special new member of the Team to help out.

Meanwhile, Dawna gets a call from Trent, wondering how the renovation is going. She wishes he were here to be with them. "Me, too," Trent answers.

The Team hasn't gotten far, however, before "paths" cross. Preston has freelanced a decision to remove a hedge without telling anyone. Contractor Dave is not amused.

"I came out here and he's throwing a chainsaw around," jokes Constance. "The only thing he was missing was a goalie's mask." Calm is quickly restored, however.

With the designers and crew working day and night, the home's metamorphosis is well under way. Constance is the main organizer, Michael and Tracy work on the furnishings and décor, and Ty works on the boys' bathroom. It's up to Paul and Trent to refinish the vanity. With only two days to go before the Woslums return, Paul takes time out to bake a cake for Michael's 40th birthday—in a neighbor's kitchen!

The landscaping is coming along well. In fact, Preston is blown away when help arrives on Day 5. The Los Angeles Dodgers groundskeeping crew arrives bearing authentic Dodger dirt, sod, and stadium seating for Preston's backyard project—a miniaturized replica of Dodger stadium!

But Preston just can't seem to avoid trouble. On Day 6, he sneaks out to buy a couch and promptly sends it through the window of his truck when he brakes too hard.

"What can I say? I'm a knucklehead. I didn't have rope with me." Amazingly, the renovation is completed and on time.

The living room, kitchen, and dining room areas have been opened up and equipped with state-of-the-art appliances and home entertainment gear. Alex's room has a castle theme with a drawbridge Murphy bed, and connects through a roll-up door to Nicholas' spaceship-themed bedroom, complete with padded walls.

The office has become Steven's room, with wall-to-wall orange shag carpet, hi-tech DVD player, and flat screen TV. The garage has been converted into a beautiful new office for Trent.

Terra cotta tiles and a warm hearth dominate the opened-up living area in the Woslums' new Spanish hacienda. No more folding table and plastic lawn chairs for dining. Now Dawna, Trent, and the boys will be surrounded by state-of-the-art home entertainment equipment. Dawna's new kitchen has the latest appliances and Trent's got a new office in the garage. Luckily, the couch doesn't seem to have suffered any damage from its rocky ride in Preston's truck!

"The week we shot this episode was the week that troops in Iraq captured Saddam Hussein. The troops that captured Saddam was Trent Woslum's outfit."

—Executive Producer Tom Forman

WELCOME TO YOUR NEW HOME!

The master bedroom has been completely redone. Its centerpiece is Dawna's treasured vanity, newly refinished.

With friends, family, and the hundreds of contractors and sub-contractors who worked on their home cheering them on, the Woslums return to their amazing new home.

They love the new house, especially the backyard that has been transformed into a mini-replica of Dodger stadium. But the biggest surprise comes when Ty reveals the identity of his special assistant.

"Dad!" the boys scream.

"This really wasn't about the house," says Paul. "It was about seeing their dad."

"It was like Christmas for everybody, man," said Ty. "It was cool."

"I was so shocked to be able to see him," recalls Dawna of the moment. "It's been so long. It was wonderful. There's...there's no way I can put it into words. Dad's home."

Preston uses his landscaping skills to turn the backyard into a mini ballfield—complete with real Los Angeles Dodgers' dirt, sod, and stadium seating. If you're the catcher, Preston, you're supposed to crouch!

Mendoza FAMILY

Social worker Contessa Mendoza knows a thing or two about rising above adversity.

Contessa was a 17-year-old high school student when her daughter Analicia, 10, was born. Despite the hurdles of being a single mom, she excelled in school, graduating as class valedictorian before putting herself through college where she earned a Master's degree.

In her job as social worker, big-hearted Contessa meets many needy and troubled families. When it comes to meeting those needs, she just can't seem to say 'No.' She has taken two other kids, her adopted son Angel, 18, and foster son Tony, 14, into her home. On weekends, her post-war tract house is overflowing with other foster kids, including the siblings of Angel and Tony.

"I've just given my entire life to the kids," says Contessa.

"CAN WE GET THE MENDOZER AND JUST PLOW THIS THING DOWN?"
—PRESTON

The Team enthusiastically agrees it's time to give something special back to Contessa.

"We're on our way, Contessa!" says Michael Moloney as Ty, Preston, Paul, Tracy, and Constance clap and cheer.

THE HOUSE

As the bus pulls to a stop in front of the Mendoza house, Ty briefs the Team on the home's many problems, including water damage and serious plumbing and electrical problems. One look at the house from the street, however, is all the Team needs to know this will be a big undertaking.

The size of the house will be their main obstacle. It's just too small. Once inside, the space problem is shocking.

"You turn left, you turn right, and that's about it," says Contessa. Everything, including the kitchen sink—it literally appears to be sinking—needs changing. Analicia's room is small, and painted a horrible dark pink.

"I hate the colors on the wall," Analicia says. The Team agrees.

A visit to Contessa's room, with its old carpeting and a mish-mash of ancient furnishings, is a virtual trip back in time.

"Hi, I'm here in 1974," jokes Michael.

Angel, a big rap and hip-hop music fan, and Tony, a budding astronomer, share a small room; each desperately wants his own room. Unfortunately, there just are not enough rooms to go around.

The worst room in the house is the bathroom. It's a disaster. The hot water handle on the tub is a pair of pliers.

The other rooms are not much better. Ty and Michael are nearly crushed trying to hold open the broken garage door. Just as well, as the garage is piled high with discarded items from the house.

"You can't even walk in here," says Ty, stumbling through the debris.

In the driveway, Contessa's old gas-guzzler sits abandoned. Angel would love to have a car, but Contessa says he can only have it once he starts earning a salary to pay for upkeep and insurance.

The backyard, which features a sadly neglected fishpond, is an important living space for Contessa and the kids, who like to camp out and barbecue to alleviate the congestion in their home.

The Team agrees on what needs to be done.

"Can we get the Mendozer and plow this thing down?" asks Preston.

THE RENOVATION BEGINS NOW!

The Mendozas are all smiles as Ty sees them off on a week's vacation to Disney World.

It's time roll up some sleeves.

"Is there any possible way we can go up?" asks Michael.

Everyone agrees that's the way to go.

Tracy, Constance, and Preston have big plans for a backyard "Camp Mendoza." Preston and Paul propose an observatory theme for Tony's room.

Constance, Tracy, and Michael will give Angel's room an urban hip-hop look, complete with a DJ booth and the "biggest, craziest speakers," says Michael. As for Contessa's room, "she's taking care of everybody else, that's her life," says Michael. "We now need to give her a place where she's going to feel pampered. I want to give her a really sophisticated, elegant, polished-looking master bedroom."

Demolition begins under the supervision of the husband -and-wife contractor team of Dave and Jodi Bagwell. Work is already behind schedule, however. Everyone is stressing out as rain threatens to delay renovation further. Luckily,

"This was the first time we had a whole series of things we told ourselves we would never do, and then went right ahead and did them anyway. We would never add square footage to a house, and we did. One thing you could never do in a week is add a second storey. And that's exactly what we did.

It was also the first time it rained. It started on the Mendoza episode and has continued for two straight years."

—Executive Producer Tom Forman

Design 101

"The problems you run into by going up two storeys is that you destroy everything below."

—Constance

the rain holds off while the concrete foundation and floors are poured.

Meanwhile, Ty—armed with his bullhorn—makes a surprise visit to Orlando and the Mendozas. They greet him with a collective "what the..." look.

"So guys, what's it going to be? The raspberry-chocolate plaid or the rust with plaid trim?"

Uhhhh.

By Day 4, framing is completed. Everything is behind schedule. Astronaut Commander Robert Curbeam drops in to lend some expertise to Tony's observatory-themed room.

The master bedroom has a four-poster bed so high that Contessa will need a ladder. Analicia's room, which Ty built with the help of the Disney Imagineers, features a recessed aquarium and a bed made with sea kelp.

It's one day to go, but the Team can't start decorating because of construction delays. Then the rain comes hammering down. When it stops, the Team pulls an all-nighter to catch up. Everyone is crashed out on floors and counters trying to steal a few winks before the last rush.

"They're coming in five hours," says a disheveled Preston. "Do I need a makeover?"

WELCOME TO YOUR NEW HOME!

The Mendozas return home to a frenetic welcome from their friends and family.

"What they did was take my taste, and do it right," says Contessa.

"I'm really happy for my mom," says Analicia. "She really gave her life up for me and my brothers and she deserves this house."

Welcome to "Camp Mendoza," complete with fish-filled streams, ponds, waterfall, and a beautiful deck and grill.

Contessa had hoped that Angel might use this car to help him get a job. But she couldn't afford repairs. Thanks to the magic of world-famous customizer George Barris—creator of the Batmobile—Angel has a new set of awesome wheels. A generous job offer from the contractor Bagwells means Angel can afford insurance, too.

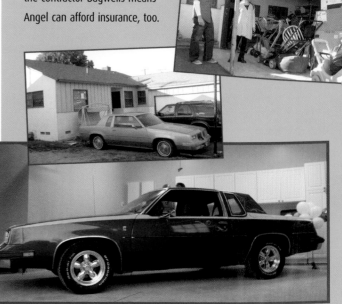

Hardin FAMILY

After more than 30 years' estrangement, Freeman Hardin Jr. set out to find his father Freeman Sr., a former heavyweight boxer and US Marine. After a long search, he found him one Father's Day, living a homeless existence on the streets of Los Angeles, and brought him back to live at the tumbledown little ranch he shared in Phelan, California, with his wife, Laura, and their 17-year-old daughter, Ashley.

The ranch, however, is small and Freeman Sr. must live in an old trailer in the yard.

"It took them this long to find their dad," says Ty. "They finally got the family back together. Our job is to get them under one roof."

THE HOUSE

The approach to the Hardin house is an opportunity for the Team—Ty, Tracy, Paige, Preston, and Alle—to enjoy the spectacular natural beauty of the desert foothills of the eastern San Gabriel Mountains.

The house—a rundown 1970s-era ranch—affords a slightly less spectacular aspect. Ty realizes its advantage is its large piece of land, "which gives us a lot of room to play."

While their house is being made over, the Hardins will be relaxing at a dude ranch resort in Arizona. There is only time for a quick tour before they are on their way. With its adobe tile roof and stucco walls, the house is a combination Spanish villa and ranch that Ty calls "Spanch."

Inside, the Team inspects the cramped living room. The badly outdated kitchen features a tiny window with a tree that blocks the view of the snow-capped peaks in the distance.

"They've got all this great land," says Preston. "If I lived here, I'd want to see those beautiful mountains."

Ashley's is a typical messy teenager's room. It's obvious she loves the color pink.

NO...SERIOUSLY.
WE **KNOW**
WHAT WE'RE
DOING...

"I DON'T SEE **HOW** THEY COULD **PULL** IT **OFF**. BUT **THEY'RE PROFESSIONALS.** I'M **NOT.**"
—HOMEOWNER FREEMAN HARDIN

The master bedroom is sparsely decorated, featuring a plastic deck chair in one corner. If the house and rooms are all on the small side, the garage is not.

It's the most logical site for expanded living space.

The last stop is the old trailer Freeman Sr. calls home.

"I'm not happy with him in this," says Freeman Jr. "I'd rather him be in the house, but this is the best we could work out. He needs his independence, but at the same time, he needs to be watched and cared for."

THE RENOVATION BEGINS NOW!

After a quick "bon voyage" to the Hardins, the Design Team is raring to go.

Paige catches the frontier spirit. She is decked out in blue jeans and pink cowboy hat. Preston, not to be outdone, uses his "excellent" John Wayne impression to exhort and encourage the Team.

The whole house, they decide, will get a ranch look.

"The Ponderosa thing," Preston calls it.

They decide to turn the main living areas into one huge open room with exposed wooden beams. Paige and Tracy are excited about Ashley's room, which they'll give a 1950s look, with plenty of pink.

The garage will be converted into a boxing-themed living area for Freeman Sr.

Just for the fun of it, Preston suggests a greenhouse. Alle has plans for a barn on the property, while Ty claims the old trailer as his secret project. He promptly climbs inside it as it is wheeled off to parts unknown.

The Team is happy to be reunited with contractor Dave Tesh and his crew. It's time to get started. Everyone keeps a wary eye on the sky, however, as snow begins to fall just as the demolition begins.

Everything about this job, it seems, will be different. The traditional yellow hard hats have been exchanged for white cowboy hats, and Ty directs the job from atop a big white horse.

"You guys ready to saddle up?" he bellows through his bullhorn. "Well, let's move 'em out people!"

Paige is photographing the entire project for a scrapbook she wants to give the Hardins. The garage is coming along nicely, but trouble breaks out when Paige and Alle relocate some trees without checking with Dave first.

It's a breach of protocol and Dave is not amused. However, the rules are rehearsed and everyone agrees to stay focused. Work resumes.

Chainsaw artist Chainsaw Jack arrives to work on some wood carvings and signs, and the greenhouse and barn start to go up.

Ty calls the Hardins with news that they'll be getting a "green house."

"I didn't really want a green house," worries Freeman Jr. "I don't like green."

With 24 hours to go, a group of the Hardins' friends and neighbors arrives to stain the barn. Inside the house, work is so far ahead of schedule that the decorators will have access to it by mid-afternoon.

All that's left is for Paige and Tracy to put the finishing touches on Ashley's room. With time to spare, the makeover is complete!

WELCOME TO YOUR NEW HOME!

A cheering crowd has gathered on the Hardin property to welcome the family home. "Move that bus!" shouts Ty.

Laura Hardin cries tears of happiness while Freeman Jr. literally jumps for joy. Even soft-spoken Freeman Sr. is truly moved.

"Oh, it's wonderful," he says.

The American West furnishings and design are spectacular. Ashley's room is a '50s rock 'n roll dream, with a blue and pink bed, retro pink couch with car fins, and jukebox in the corner. The master bedroom is western classy. But Freeman Sr.'s huge new room is best of all, with its mural, boxing equipment, and connected modern bathroom. Now he has his own comfortable space he can call his own. And the junior Freeman loves his greenhouse.

"I was feeling week to my knees you know," Freeman Jr. says. "This house is so beautiful, but it means so much more when you can share it with those you love."

Ty Pennington

He may play the jokester on the show, but Ty is no slouch with the toolbox. He financed his college education with his carpentry skills and is owner and chief designer of his online furniture company, Furniture Unlimited.

Each week on *Extreme Makeover: Home Edition,* dozens of fans—mothers, grandmothers, toddlers, and teens—stand by desperately hoping to catch a glimpse of Ty Pennington, the sometimes off-the-wall hunk-of-a-carpenter, in action. Beyond cracking jokes, though, he really does enjoy designing and building, working with contractors and designers though the numerous challenges that arise—and sometimes conflicting personalities that clash—to create magical homes for deserving families.

Ty, who dubs his school of design "modern primitive," says it's the creative process that motivates him. Whether he is designing interiors, building furniture, creating a line of home fashions, or playing a funny song on the guitar, it's putting the "fun" in "function" that keeps him going.

First known as the playful carpenter on *Trading Spaces,* Pennington has signed an exclusive multi-year agreement with Sears, partnering with them in a broad range of activities, including product design and development, merchandising and advertising, and serving as ambassador for the Sears American Dream Campaign.

A self-proclaimed "Jack of all Trades, Master of None," Pennington can add author to his vast list of skills: His first book, *Ty's Tricks,* published by Hyperion in 2003, was a bestseller.

Pennington spent most of his childhood in Atlanta. Following high school, he attended Kennesaw College, focusing on art and history. After one year, his art professor suggested a career in graphic design, so he started working as a carpenter by day and attending classes at the Atlanta Art Institute by night. After graduation he continued his education at the Atlanta College of Art, studying painting and sculpture while honing his carpentry skills to pay for his education.

During his final semester, Pennington was approached by a modeling scout and soon began an exciting and lucrative career. He traveled the world and appeared in numerous magazine ads and television commercials.

Pennington has appeared on the covers and pages of numerous publications. He was recently on the cover of *TV Guide,* has been one of *People* magazine's "Sexiest Men Alive" and "Most Eligible Bachelors," and was also on *Entertainment Weekly*'s "It List."

23

We Get Mail!

It may seem hard to believe.

A complete home makeover in only seven days? That's crazy!

But what is equally crazy is what happens way before the Design Team and its huge traveling crew and production staff ever arrive at a house to begin renovation. It takes a gigantic effort from a horde of people and hundreds and hundreds of hours of preparation before the first camera can ever start rolling.

For instance, according to Family Casting Director Charisse Simonian, her team receives about 15 bins each week, filled to the brim with applications from families who want to be featured on *Extreme Makeover: Home Edition.*

That translates into about 15,000 applications each week!

Simonian and her staff of eight open and read each and every application. If they are interested, and the application comes accompanied with a tape, they will watch the family on tape. But not all applications come with tapes or photos, so if the team is interested in a family, they then have to call and request additional information.

But that's only the beginning. It doesn't mean the family has made the cut.

A conference is held to discuss contenders. Then tapes and pictures are edited to create a one-page synopsis on the families that meet selection criteria. Simonian estimates maybe one family out of that original 15,000 will make the cut! She signs off on a family about once every two to three weeks.

The casting video and write-up then move up the ladder for approval. What are they looking for? Simonian says the family must have a compelling story. They should be likable and empathetic, and must require or need a makeover, and deserve one as well. "We like families who help other people."

Winnowing down that huge volume of applications is a daunting process that can take up to three weeks of intense work.

Some of the applications, she admits, are quite...creative. "We get bribed with candy, popcorn, home-made cakes and pies. It doesn't affect our decision, though."

COX FAMILY

John Cox doesn't just have a job; he has a calling, helping young people, churches, and other organizations across America. With his work as a youth pastor taking him all over the country, John and his wife Wendy have lived in nine different places over the last 10 years. To complicate matters, money has been tight since Wendy quit her job as a nurse to stay home and care for the couple's three daughters, Shaina, 14, Hannah, 8, and Nicole, 3.

In 2002, after country-music-loving John took a permanent position as a youth minister with a nearby church, he and Wendy purchased their first house in Simi Valley, California. Unfortunately, the house needed far more work than they could afford to tackle on John's modest salary.

This is a family devoted to helping others. Now it's time someone helped them out.

THE HOUSE

"Good morning, Cox family! Wake up and come on out here!"

The family scrambles out the front door, eyes wide in disbelief, and waves to the many neighbors who have gathered to share in their excitement.

John cannot believe the Team is actually standing in his driveway. Ty informs the family that while the home is being renovated, they will be spending the week at Disney World. First, Ty and the Team need a tour. From Michael's immediate reaction, the Team knows it faces a major challenge.

The family admits that the house has gone from fixer-upper to major-downer.

"The best way to explain our feeling is, shock, awe, disbelief, overjoyed, elated, blessed, undeserving, overwhelmed, excited, ecstatic, thrilled, receptive, relaxed, happy, peaceful. I can't believe this has really happened to us!" —John Cox

The house itself is a small bungalow with a stucco exterior. Inside, the ceilings are low and the furnishings are a veritable hodgepodge of thrift store chic. In fact, the Cox' theme for their home is "Rescue it, prime it, paint it." The living room, kitchen, and dining room areas have a cold, utilitarian white tile floor. The largest area is the garage, but it's a disaster. The family loves music, but their instruments are scattered and buried under all the boxes and junk.

The backyard has a nice in-ground swimming pool. But a cantilevered overhand has been painted a rather vibrant blue the neighbors dubbed the "Smurf house." Michael looks to be in shock.

Nothing outside or inside the house seems to work, either. Concrete walks, fences, and gates are broken. The girls' bathroom has no showerhead. But it's the perfect shower, Preston remarks, if you're 8 inches tall and fit under the faucet. Wendy demonstrates how the shower door in the master bathroom won't close properly.

"You can tell the houses that need a little love," says Ty. "And this one needed a lot of love."

Uh...kay

"I just think we ought to give them the bus. I mean, this is the modern-day Partridge Family. Could they get any closer?"

—Preston

WHEN THEMES COLLIDE

"I'M NOT GOING TO SABOTAGE THEIR ROOMS. BUT I MIGHT MESS WITH THEIR HEADS A LITTLE BIT."

—MICHAEL

"DOING THIS IS HALF LIKE GOING TO CAMP AND HALF LIKE GOING TO WAR."

—CONTRACTOR MATT

THE RENOVATION STARTS NOW

The Team sketches out a plan. They agree to go up. Constance volunteers to work with the contractors on a "great room" featuring open space and a high ceiling. They come up with a fabulous idea to convert the garage into an ultra-sophisticated studio where the family can play music together. Paul, Preston, and Michael notice that daughter Shaina has plastered a bumpersticker across her door:

"Skateboarding is Not a Crime!"

They decide to give her new bedroom the full skater treatment, including a half-pipe along one wall and shelves and drawer faces constructed from real skateboards. Hannah and Nicole love to play dress-up, so Tracy and Constance propose a new bedroom with a magical diva dressing-room theme.

The guys promise they will build the best and coolest bedroom. "No way," Constance and Paige counter. The two camps make a bet. The losers will make and serve dinner to the winners. On his return, Ty chooses a section of backyard, which he dubs Tyland, as his personal mystery project.

On Day 3, demolition is complete and the framing begins. It's time for Tracy and Constance to begin work on the "ultimate

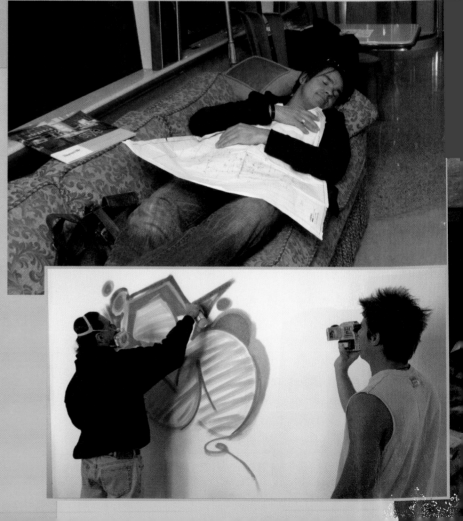

theater diva dressing room," but it's not long before things start to go awry. Constance appears to be cracking under pressure, mainly because of her plan for overly complicated folding bunk beds in the little girls' room.

The contractors have made exceptional progress, with walls of sheetrock already in place, the kitchen cabinets already installed, and siding going up outside. The real question at this point is whether or not the Design Team can keep up with the construction crew. Ty worries that the "bet" is sidetracking them from more important tasks.

At 4 A.M. on Day 5, the "smackdown" contest between the guys and the gals spirals out of control, and Ty decides to step in and call off the bet. He buys the tired and hungry Team pizza as a victory present for both sides.

"And here's the good news," he says. "You can grab a slice of pizza and actually put a paintbrush in the other hand. So grab a slice, grab a paintbrush, and let's finish that house."

With not much time left, nerves are raw and things become a bit hectic.

"We've got this house to paint," worries Ty.

"We got to build this whole thing tonight. Everybody is tired. No one has had any sleep. Paul hasn't slept in three days. Everyone is getting a little edgy.

"Paul just snaps on Constance. And I was like, 'Dude, you know? Like, just chill. Let's not, you know, kill each other. Not yet.'"

After a flurry of last-minute activity on the morning of Day 7, the house is finally finished. Just in time, as the limousine with the Cox family pulls down the street with hundreds of friends and neighbors cheering them home.

"Hey bus driver, hit it!" Ty hollers. The bus pulls away and the Cox family literally jumps for joy at the sight of their new home.

It's more than John can believe. "That's not our home!"

Tyland turns out to be a cool tropical beach scene, with a tiki hut, spa, humongous barbeque, and the "new" pool with large boulders and a working waterfall. Finally, Ty leads the Coxes to the garage, now a digital recording studio decked out with start-of-the-art recording equipment and musical instruments. After an impromptu jam with John on guitar and Shaina on drums, Ty rolls up a door revealing an outdoor amphitheater. Tonight, the Cox house is a packed house, with country music superstar LeAnn Rimes sitting in the front row!

Rimes sings a beautiful *a cappella* version of "Amazing Grace," joined in the second verse by the family, Design Team and crew, friends, and neighbors.

"I feel blessed," says Wendy, "extremely blessed and grateful."

It's been a very tense—and intense—seven-day makeover, but from the reaction from John and the rest of the Cox family, it looks like all the hard work was worth it.

"That's not our house!" *It is.*

LOOK WHO DROPPED BY!

"That rocks! That rocks! Oh my gosh! That's LeAnn Rimes!" John Cox is blown away when the country music superstar generously shows up to inaugurate their family music room.

"I mean, to see her there was...that was like, one of the greatest experiences of my life," says John.

"To see this country superstar, being so sweet and humble," adds Wendy, "sharing this moment. It was heartfelt."

"We were truly amazed at the inlay in the granite on the island and the walls of the kitchen," says John. "They have fulfilled our wildest dreams. The girls just love their rooms. It is a sanctuary for them. It's a place of refuge for our family."

McCrory FAMILY

PAIGE
HEMMIS'
1ST SHOW

"You're giving me the opportunity to be the father that I want to be to my kids. To be present for them, and to listen to them, and be awake and alive to actually raise them."

—Thomas McCrory

Tom and Deirdre McCrory's home in Costa Mesa, California, is one of the nicest the Team has ever taken on. It's also one of the smallest.

That's the big problem.

The McCrorys lived happily in a lovely little tract house with their two sons, Rory, 3, and 21-month-old Connor.

Deirdre had some big news, however. She was pregnant. With triplets!

Tom and Deirdre admit that panic set in. Their home was already too small. When Grandma Marie McCrory arrived from Ireland to help Deirdre, space was further compromised. Three adults and two rambunctious boys—with three more kids on the way!

It was chaos. Not to mention the obvious financial implications.

Tom had no choice but to start looking for a second job to pay for a larger house or an addition on their existing one. Maybe even uprooting and moving out of state.

But that meant being a no-show father to his children.

"I don't want to be the guy who just shows up to pay the bills," explains Tom. "Part of what would be so incredible for us as a family is just being able to be together. What you guys are giving us is the ability to remodel our future. You're giving me the opportunity to be the father I want to be to my kids."

THE HOUSE

With Connie, Tracy, and Paul still recovering from the last makeover, the Design Team heads to the makeover site with some new faces on board: Paige Hemmis, a carpenter, and Alle Ghadban, responsible for building and planning.

And Michael introduces perhaps the most important member of the Team: Ricky the Design Dog, Michael's pet pooch.

No, Paige has not lost a contact. The Team meets to plan a strategy for the renovation. With five people in the tiny house already, and three babies on the way, Ty does the math.

"Five. Then we have three in there. My question is: Where are you going to put these kids?"

He thinks.

"This is crazy."

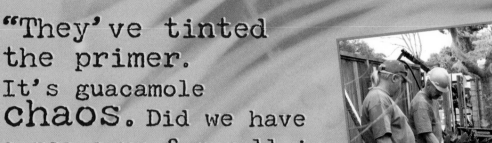

WORRIED? WHO...ME?

"They've tinted the primer. It's guacamole **chaos.** Did we have a pea-soup fog roll in this morning?"

—Michael

When the bus pulls up in front of the house, the Team is in total agreement "It's a very nice looking house," comments Preston.

"But there are four in the house," says Ty. "And it's about to be seven. Well, with Grandma, eight."

"Wow!"

Ty booms into his bullhorn, "Good morning, McCrory family!"

The McCrorys are thrilled! Especially when they learn they will wait out the seven-day extreme makeover relaxing at a luxurious spa and resort in Arizona. But first, Ty asks them to take the Team on a quick tour.

"So I like the basic design of the house," says Ty.

"It's not bad," admits Tom, "for a shoebox."

The house features an open-concept living room, dining room, and kitchen area. The master bedroom is bland and messy. To demonstrate its ridiculously small size, Ty stands in the shower. He invites Deirdre to join him.

Deirdre jokes that now she can tell all her friends she has been in the shower with Ty.

In little Connor's room, Ty joins in as the toddler shows off his incredible jumping abilities. There, we learn of Connor's love of animals—stuffed and real. In

his room, 3-year-old Rory, decked out in a striped shirt and pirate hat, confesses his love for all things Captain Hook.

Back outside, Ty tours the garage, which has been hastily and not-too-sumptuously—converted into living quarters for Grandma Marie.

The Team agrees that this is a different kind of makeover project.

"I think this family's different because they're not needy," says Michael, "they are suddenly in need."

With the lack of space obvious to one and all, the Team agrees that a large extension is an absolute must.

"We're expanding your house to match Deirdre's giant stomach," says Preston. No small task!

THE RENOVATION BEGINS NOW!

As the McCrorys pack for their vacation, the Team sits down to plan the makeover. Alle takes the lead, proposing a 500-square-foot extension off the back of the house for two extra bedrooms and a huge nursery for the new babies. Michael and Paige propose a pirate theme for Rory's room and a jungle theme for Connor's.

The Team is facing a unique design problem. For the nursery, is it blue or pink?

"This was the first time that Preston Sharp and Michael Moloney shopped for furniture," remembers Coordinating Producer Diane Korman. "The first...and the last."

Ty calls Tom. The McCrorys don't know, so Ty asks if it's OK if he finds out himself.

"If you guys want to find out, you guys are welcome to," says Tom.

Back at the planning table, Ty tells the designers he'll be making the garage his secret project. "I'm going to be shacking up in Grandma's room," he says. His project, as usual, is shrouded in secrecy. "But I can tell you this," he says, "it will not be kid-oriented."

Ty films the demolition portion of the renovation for his D-day message to the vacationing McCrorys. "So, let's tear this house apart," he shouts as the sledgehammer- and crowbar-wielding crew assaults the house. In the middle of a chaotic scene, with walls being demolished and the house seemingly reduced to a pile of rubble, a wild-eyed Ty tells the shell-shocked McCrorys to "Relax, everything's under control."

As the new kid on the block, Alle appears a bit unprepared for demolition.

"Alle, dude," jokes Ty. "You look like you are going out for martinis!"

Unfortunately, fitting in is not just an issue of wearing the right clothes. Alle conceives of his job on the project as making all the decisions. The veteran members of the Team know only too well how important compromise and teamwork is.

Day 2 is almost done and the hallway leading to the new wing is already framed and the concrete floor is poured. A good days' work, Ty concludes. Meanwhile, Michael—with the sex of the babies a mystery—is wondering how to decorate the nursery.

IT'S 11:59: DO YOU KNOW WHERE YOUR NEW HOME IS?

"We've got four hours until the family gets home. We're in trouble"

—Ty

There he is!

Exhausted crew track down Ty and his bullhorn and "escort" him off site.

Not really. Truthfully, the crew loves Ty's booming bullhorn reminders of how far behind they are. Right!!

Framing is completed on Day 3. The electrical wiring is run; the roof is finished, and the walls are insulated. Even the air conditioning is installed. Out front, the energetic and very organized Paige is cutting the numerous animal pieces for the jungle room with a jigsaw.

While Ty slaves away on his mysterious secret room, Michael calls the McCrorys with an update. He offers them the opportunity to ask a member of the Design Team anything they want about the renovation. The joke is on them, though, when the designer in question turns out to be none other than Ricky the Design Dog.

His lighthearted mood evaporates, however, on Day 4 when he discovers that the color of the house doesn't match the paint color he chose.

"They've tinted the primer. It's guacamole chaos," he says.

"Did a pea soup fog roll in this morning?" asks Preston. Michael solves the problem himself with a trip to the paint store.

The house is painted and the courtyard is tiled. The landscaping, however, is lagging behind. On Day 5, there is still lots to do. In the nursery, work is at a standstill as Michael waits—and frets—about the sex of the babies.

Paige has her hands full, too, with hundreds and hundreds of jigsawed pieces for the jungle room, all of which need to be painted and assembled.

Preston comes to her aid by going door to door to organize a neighborhood paint party. The many friends and neighbors of the McCrorys are only too happy to oblige, and the painting begins.

To Michael's immense relief, Ty returns from his conference with Deirdre's doctor with news. Work on the nursery kicks into high gear. Unfortunately, just when the Team needs Michael the most, he falls desperately ill.

Unwilling to let the Team down, however, he communicates directions for the interior furnishing to the rest of the Team via walkie-talkie from inside the bus, flat on his back.

"Roger, Prester one-niner," he mutters groggily to an exhausted Preston.

It's chaos and confusion. But with everyone's incredible patience and hard work, somehow it gets done.

With scant hours left before the family returns, Preston is busy assembling a patio table. Michael, still not 100 percent, is back on his feet and directing a team of "neighbor ladies" in the new nursery.

WELCOME TO YOUR NEW HOME!

Rain threatens the homecoming.

But as a huge crowd of umbrella-toting friends attest, it could not ruin the spirit and joy of the day. With family and neighbors lining the rain-soaked street, the McCrorys return to a jubilant welcome.

The awestruck family members open the front door to their new dream home. It's beyond their wildest dreams. The living room fireplace—a totally child-friendly innovation—throws heat but has no flame. Tom and the family are dumbstruck.

"It's a hologram!" explains Ty. "You can literally stick your hand inside, but nobody will ever get burned."

Rory's pirate room features a giant ship bed, a treasure chest toy box, and a huge "Rory's Treasure Map" painted on one wall. Connor's jungle room is filled with stuffed animals large and small. Its centerpiece is a frog bed—just the right size for a two-year-old—and Connor immediately starts bouncing up and down on it. A boy's seal of approval!

Outside, Ty shows Tom the garage, which he has converted into "McCrory's Pub." It's a sports-themed bar complete with pool table, a dart board, and several televisions.

"This is mind-blowing," says Tom. "My buddies are going to die."

Grandma Marie is thrilled with the new guest bedroom, which features a lovely mantelpiece made by Deirdre that the Design Team was extra careful to save. Perched upon it are the ultrasound images of the triplets.

The couple's new master bedroom and bathroom are so luxurious. "I feel like I died and woke up in first class," Tom says.

Back outside, the backyard is a virtual kids' paradise, with "the biggest playground we could find," Ty says, and a quiet area for Deirdre, complete with a babbling brook.

"This is like the Garden of Eden," she says.

Of course, Tom and Deirdre know that what awaits them is the new nursery. And the answer to a dream.

Tom confides, "You know, Deirdre, she's hoping so much for a daughter." Deirdre is not disappointed. She opens the door to find three cribs: blue, pink, and blue!

"Thank you God, we have a girl," she says.

Rain cannot dampen the joy of the McCrorys when they first set eyes on their new—much bigger—home.

Michael, meanwhile, does some last minute shopping blue for boys, pink for girls—he hopes.

WE'RE NOT DONE YET...

"I'm afraid I'm giving bird legs to a giraffe." —Paige

Despite some early jitters, new-kid-on-the-block Paige does a fabulous job creating an animal-themed bedroom that is a child's dream come true.

The Team made sure to provide plenty of new parking for the triplets.

Meanwhile, preparing dinner for a big family should be a bit less chaotic in this spacious, open-style kitchen with state-of-the-art appliances.

BEFORE

WE'RE NOT DONE YET!

MCCRORY 3

It's a girl...and a boy...and a boy.

If Tom and Deirdre ever have a chance to relax, they can do it in style in this sleek and very modern living room.

Harris
FAMILY

'Sweet' Alice Harris welcomes the Team to her home and her community. "She's trying to open doors of opportunty for everybody who lives in this community."

Alice Harris has spent a lifetime helping others. But when a freak rainstorm badly flooded her home, 'Sweet' Alice, as she is known to everyone in her Watts neighborhood in South Los Angeles, needed some help of her own.

On November 17, 2003, the worst storm in 100 years dumped 5 inches of rain and hail in less than two hours over South L.A., including Watts, an impoverished neighborhood known for its infamous riots and high unemployment and crime rates.

Thousands of houses, businesses, and schools were flooded with rain and filthy backed-up sewer water, including the home of longtime community activist Alice Harris, a Watts resident for over 40 years. In the 1960s, 'sweet' Alice founded Parents of Watts (POW), an organization feeding and sheltering the poor and homeless and providing many other programs for those in need of assistance of all kinds. In the 1980s, 'sweet' Alice started collecting and distributing toys for needy children at Christmas time. And every Thanksgiving, she is known to cook dinner for up to 400 homeless people in her small kitchen and on four rusty old gas grills in her front yard.

THE HOME

"It's not exactly Pleasantville, guys," explains Ty as the *Extreme Makeover: Home Edition* bus turns the corner and rolls up to the Harris house. "And I think a lot of people are quite frightened of it, to be honest with you."

Tracy, Constance, Paul—plus new Team member, landscape designer Dawson Connor—agree. The neighborhood needs a lot of love. They all agree that this project is above and beyond.

'Sweet' Alice deserves nothing less.

"Good morning, Harris family!" bellows Ty.

'Sweet' Alice, her husband Alan and their grandson Warwick, 14, come to the door. They clap and cheer, not believing they have been selected for an extreme makeover.

Ty announces that they'll be relaxing at a beach resort near San Diego during the seven days their house is being made over.

And what a makeover it's going to be.

The floodwater—Alice explains that the water came up to her knees—has soaked and seeped into everything.

The Team notices some eye-popping structural damage. The cement floor in the dining room has a huge crack, and the kitchen cabinets are rotted through. The bedrooms are essentially empty. All the furniture has been destroyed. Warwick, a jazz music fan and straight-A student, is sleeping on a mattress on the floor, his clothing stuffed into garbage bags.

At the back of the house, Alice shows Ty the back porch she closed in as a type of dorm room for the many family members and guests who frequently visit. The backyard, with its piles of discarded furniture and other ruined household items, is mostly concrete.

"I really would like to be able to sit back here in the evening and relax," 'Sweet' Alice says.

To help make that dream come true, Ty wishes them well on their much needed and much deserved vacation.

Grandson Warwick and husband Alan pose with Alice. In her community, she is a tireless amabassador of hope and opportunity to anyone in need.

"This was the first episode that we really gelled as a team," recalls Supervising Producer Michael Maloy, "and realized what our mission was."

THE RENOVATION BEGINS NOW!

It's time for the Team to plot its makeover strategy. First, open up the kitchen. The strategy is nothing succeeds like excess. Paul wants to build a giant dining room table "that seats like 60 people," but is brought back to earth and settles on 12. The Team proposes a jazz theme for Warwick's room.

"I say we get an old piano and maybe cut it in half—enough to put a bed in there," says Paul.

With the Team talking makeover, Ty tours the neighborhood on foot.

"Wow, man, this neighborhood could use some help," he says. "Alice isn't the only one hit by this flood. She's in love with her neighborhood. I feel like her dream is to makeover the neighborhood, not just her house."

The Team comes up with a plan. The whole house will get a new roof. The exterior will be done up in American Heritage style. The main living areas and master bedroom will be given a classic 1940s look. Constance wants to literally do magic by transforming little Ashley's room into Fairy Princess Land.

Ty decides the back porch dorm room will be his special project.

Contractor Matt Plaskoff and his crew are fired up to give 'Sweet' Alice and her family the makeover they deserve. Alice's daughter Livinia borrows Ty's bullhorn to call the crew to action.

"OK, guys, I want you to tear my Mom's house down."

Livinia joins Ty to record his D-day message.

"Hi Mom!" shouts Livinia as the house—literally—crashes down around her. "I had nothing to do with this. It was Ty's idea!"

The concrete is poured, and by Day 3, the framing for Ty's back porch dorm room is just about done. Ty is on his hands ands knees stripping what seem like a dozen old doors.

Later, Sears' American Dream Campaign Team drops by with a gift for the neighborhood: a tractor trailer load of mattresses and bedding for the flood victims. Paul and a team of Sears representatives go door to door repairing broken appliances and handing out gift certificates.

Unbelievably, work is halted by rain!

The Team and crew have to scramble to protect the site. It's a surreal scene as the water climbs higher and higher. Luckily, Day 5 dawns with clearing skies. Work resumes at a frantic pace.

Only to be halted—again—when with a mere 24 hours to go the rain begins falling again.

No way!

¡Knew That...

Constance: Hey, Ty!

Ty: I like it. What is it?

Constance: A tree.

IT'S 11:59: DO YOU KNOW WHERE YOUR NEW HOME IS?

Ty: This neighborhood was destroyed by a flood, and we're trying to rebuild the neighborhood and the house...and it starts to rain. It's coming down pretty good now.

I Knew That... Part 2

Constance: That's the bed, Ty.

Ty: It's kind of...different.

Constance: It's very extreme. It's a round bed that suspends from the ceiling. And it floats.

Ty: Oh jeez.

Constance: It's a little pod! A little fairy princess and the pea.

Ty: A little strange. But it's nice. Well done. Carry on.

But the rain stops and the work kicks back into high gear. Especially when Ty blows away the Team by riding down the street, bullhorn in hand, on the back of a trailer toting a monstrous surprise.

"Clear the way! We've got the biggest, baddest, most extreme barbecue this side of the Mississippi!" he bellows. "It's come halfway across the country, and we're putting it in Alice's front yard."

Landscaper Dawson is...well...surprised. "This looks like a truck, dude! Over my dead body is this thing going in here."

That night, with the family due back in a matter of hours and the dining room table still not built, Paul comes down with a bad case of the flu. Tracy and Matt Plaskoff, however, track down a table at the community center that Alice assures them is theirs to use. Crisis averted!

By morning, they have a beautiful new dining room table. Awesome! Dawson is claiming victory, too. The "huge honkin' ugly smoker" barbecue seems to be nowhere to be seen.

WELCOME TO YOUR NEW HOME!

Alice Harris is special.

So it is no surprise that more than a few neighbors and friends and special guests turn out to honor her and her family upon their return. It's a very special day.

A gospel choir sets the tone. The hundreds of well-wishers crowding the street join in on the festive and joyous mood. There are huge grins all around when the family discovers that the whole neighborhood has been freshly landscaped.

"We wanted to give back to the neighborhood like Alice and her family has done, and see if we couldn't help out a little bit." —Ty

Ominously, the project is plagued by rain throughout. But the project is finished and even rain on the unveiling day cannot ruin the joy Alice and her family experience seeing their beautifiul new home.

"I can't believe they brought Beverly Hills to Watts," says Alan.

In addition to the landscaping, Ty tells Alice that her makeover includes new computers for the school she runs. The local basketball court has been resurfaced and refitted with brand new equipment. Alice is overwhelmed.

Now it's time for the unveiling.

Ty leads Alice inside her new home. 'Sweet' Alice breaks down. "I just never thought nobody would do this, to give us this down in Watts," she says as tears fill her eyes. "I just didn't believe it. And now I got what everybody in the magazines and TV have."

Dawson and the landscape team have designed a serene Zen garden where Alice can relax.

A beautiful flagstone walkway leads to "Alice's Toy Shop," a new shed packed to the rafters with hundreds of new toys to replace the ones destroyed by floodwater.

Always giving and never taking, Alice gathers friends and neighbors around her new truck-sized cooker to share the bounty. It's a beautiful moment. Even Dawson— luxuriating in the fragrant aroma of barbecue—is only too happy to admit defeat.

Amazingly, all Alice can think about is helping people —of doing more for others.

"It'll make me do more to help people. I'll never stop. I'm going to continue to do what I'm doing. This is what makes the world a better place. God will bless you," she says. "He has blessed me."

"The smoker arrived all the way from Philadelphia and it took three days. It was so late when it arrived we had to forklift the thing over the new fence and on top of the new landscaping and Ty was literally in the house hugging Alice. They were about to come outside and we were still trying to leverage the thing in place and jumped back over the fence just seconds before Ty made the 'reveal.'" —Executive Producer Tom Forman

Zitek-Gil FAMILY

The Zitek-Gil family home in Ventura, California, is a nice, big tri-level house in a good neighborhood. But for the family's eldest son, 22-year-old Robert Gil, the house is a virtual prison.

Paralyzed from the chest down after a horrific automobile accident, wheelchair-bound Robert is confined to the bottom level of the house and the converted rec room that is now his bedroom. He hasn't even been upstairs, where his bedroom used to be, for years. Not since the accident.

What It's All About:

"I got so much things on my chest I need to get off. I held my tears in, but inside, I was going crazy. Damn, this is great."

—Robert Gil

The three-storey house is a nightmare. Too many stairs. No ramps. Narrow hallways and corners that are too tight. Tables and cupboards are too high. Nothing is accessible. A trip to the bathroom is an ordeal.

Even a quick stop in the kitchen for a glass of water or a snack is a tortuous odyssey for Robert. Everything is out of reach. Routine things, like a simple family meal or grabbing a jacket from a hall closet, are just a memory.

He can't even enter his home by the front door.

Despite the difficulties he faces every day, however, Robert is not about to quit.

"Just because this happened to me, am I supposed to give up?" he says. "Nah, it's not me."

THE HOUSE

The bus pulls up in front of the Zitek-Gil home. The *EM:HE* Design Team members—Ty, Constance, Paul, Michael, and Dawson—know exactly what they need to do. "We need to give Robert his freedom back."

Since Robert is unable to use the front door, the Team sneaks around to the back of the house to surprise the Zitek-Gils.

"Good morning, Zitek-Gil family!"

Mom Pat, stepfather Lon Zitek, Robert, sister Nisha Gil, and little brother Andrew Zitek react with hugs and kisses and shouts of joy.

The family members are ecstatic to have been chosen for a makeover. Ty informs them they will be forced to sweat out the makeover on a private island in the Bahamas. They seem willing to make the sacrifice.

"I'm sure you've got some ideas about what you'd like to have done to the house," Ty wonders.

Robert nods emphatically. "You bet your ass I do!"

This cracks up the Team.

It's an eye-opening tour. The Team has to completely rethink the way they do things. They have to look at the world—not from the eye level they are used to—but from Robert's perspective.

But they are fired up for the challenge.

The trick will be meeting Robert's needs but realizing that other people in the family have needs, too.

It's obvious, for instance, that 13-year-old Andrew loves cars. Nisha's room doubles as Lon's home office. She has no privacy, and her bed must compete with fax machines and filing cabinets. Not exactly a teenaged girl's ideal situation.

The master bedroom is big. But it needs a major facelift, and a new bed.

The Team has a challenge: it's function meets form. They need to come up a plan for a house that is special-needs accessible, but that is also a home for the whole family.

THE RENOVATION BEGINS NOW!

With the Zitek-Gils heading to the Bahamas, it's time for the Team to get to work.

"We've got to get him on every floor," Paul tells Michael. The Team agrees. "He's got to be able to go everywhere I can go. Elevator. Just put an elevator in."

The Team fleshes out the plan. But it all comes back to one important innovation.

"Come hell or high water, there will be an elevator in this house seven days from now," says Michael.

There may be one problem, however.

"Get your checkbook Ty," warns Michael. The Team is justifiably concerned with the staggering construction costs.

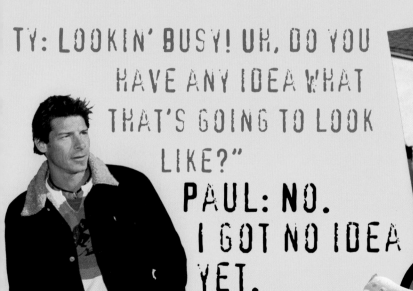

NO...SERIOUSLY. WE KNOW WHAT WE'RE DOING...

TY: LOOKIN' BUSY! UH, DO YOU HAVE ANY IDEA WHAT THAT'S GOING TO LOOK LIKE?"
PAUL: NO. I GOT NO IDEA YET.
TY: PERFECT!

Robert's room will be made over as a huge loft, complete with a kitchen and bathroom customized for his needs. The main kitchen will be redesigned. Robert's old room will be converted into Lon's new office.

As part of the master bedroom makeover, a new spa tub will be installed.

Husband and wife contractors Dave and Judy Bagwell are back, and lead a crew of 100 through the traditional Day 2 demolition job. Michael Moloney is truly inspired, swinging a sledgehammer with abandon as Ty records the demolition day message for the Ziteks-Gils.

"The man is a menace with a sledgehammer," Ty says.

Deciding that much is worth saving, Constance has decided to rescue the kitchen cabinets, sinks, sections of flooring, and other material from demolition. It will be donated to Habitat for Humanity, an organization that builds homes for needy families.

Renovation begins. Michael is touring Robert's room, which is progressing nicely.

"My primary goal is to make this house universally accessible," he says. "But that doesn't mean that it can't be fabulous." The elevator shaft is coming along well, too. The workers have started building the shaft, the sub-floor has been dug, and the foundation poured.

"This is the biggest thing we've ever done for anybody," Michael says.

"We will not fail with this elevator," says Paul. "It will work, even if I have to stand outside and pull up and down on the rope."

Unfortunately, optimistic talk is not getting the elevator built fast enough. Ty is distressed to learn the Team and crew is a full day behind schedule. The crew is working overtime. Exhaustion is taking its toll. At one point, Michael finds an exhausted Dave Bagwell asleep at his desk. He checks Dave into a hotel with instructions that the contractor not be disturbed. Just in case, Michael confiscates his cell phone, walkie-talkie, and wallet.

No way Dave is getting out of that room until he gets some sleep!

Technicians install a battery of state-of-the-art automated systems for Robert. By the morning of Day 5, the elevator is finally installed and functional.

It's been a major pain in the neck in terms of installation. They are dangerously behind schedule. Ty attempts to unwind with a "test drive" in Robert's new temperature-controlled therapy pool.

With 24 hours to go, however, there is anxious concern among Team members.

The backyard appears far from ready. Dawson assures Ty the landscaping will be ready on time. With six hours to go, the house is a beehive of frenetic activity.

And a horrible discovery: Michael's dining room table has arrived and it's four feet too long for the room. Luckily, Paul improvises by literally cutting the too-long table down to size and refinishing just in time for the chandelier to be hung in advance of the family's return.

Whew!

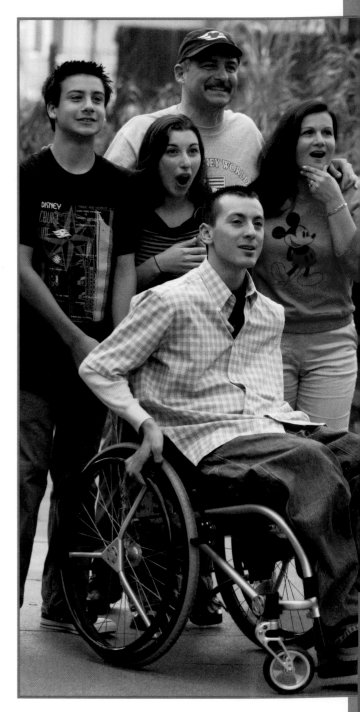

WELCOME TO YOUR NEW HOME!

The most amazing feature of the home is the complete wheelchair access of the entire home. Robert is free to go where he wants whenever he wants. He only needs to press the "magic" button and he can go anywhere he wishes. Our outlook towards life has soared since the makeover. Exciting, optimistic, and forward looking would be words to describe our feelings about our lives today."
—Lon Zitek

The Zitek-Gils return to a heartwarming welcome from friends and family chanting, "Robert! Robert! Robert!" A giant blue curtain blocks the family's view of the house.

"Drop that curtain!" shouts Ty.

The first thing Robert sees is the wooden ramp leading up to the front door of the house. "Robert can finally go through the front door for the first time in two years," says Ty.

"One miracle after another," Robert says of the renovation.

When Ty reveals the elevator, every family member is amazed. Soon, Robert is riding up to the top floor of his home for the first time in two-and-a-half years. "I forgot what it looked like," he says.

Finally able to travel the house freely via the new elevator, Robert gives his enthusiastic approval to every detail. Pat and Lon are thrilled with their new bedroom and bathroom, too. Andrew has the room of his dreams, and Nisha is moved to tears by her new, beautifully appointed bedroom. And not a fax machine in sight!

"If words could express what I was thinking," says Robert, "there'd be some crazy new words in the dictionary."

"I'm so happy to see him smiling," says Nisha. "He hasn't smiled that much since I don't know how long."

"Life can't get any better than this right now," says Robert. "It's like a dream come true. It's like being in a fairy tale."

**"Robert has cut a CD,"
says Supervising Producer
Michael Maloy.
"It's amazing. The weird
thing is, I've been playing
drums for 20 years and
the kid has more rhythm
than me after only 6 months."**

"My primary goal is to make this house universally accessible, but that does not mean it can't be FABULOUS. I'm trying to give him the world. I want this to feel like a home, not an institution. All this is for Robert."

—Andrew Lipson

"I know that it was a lifting of his spirits that has been the most important change. The elevator, endless pool, sound equipment, voice activation equipment, hardwood floors, ramp and new wheelchair, along with many letters from around the world regarding the show have contributed to Robert's new attitude towards life. This has been a priceless gift."
—Lon Zitek

Constance RAMOS

The road took her from her hometown of Kansas City, Missouri, to New York City and then across the country to Los Angeles, but Constance Ramos finally ended up with her dream job—and the man of her dreams because of it.

For the *EM:HE* producers, Constance must seem like a dream come true, too. She's an architect with a passion and talent for acting, singing, and dancing.

Constance spent her formative years at the elbow of her architect father, Chris Ramos, working summers in his successful firm.

"It was fun because I got to watch him draw and listen to him talk about design and philosophy and the things that he thought were beautiful," Constance says. "And an architect starts by just dreaming on paper, you know, they just start swirls and lines and lay out their dreams, and I was there for that part. It was always very exciting for me."

In addition to her love of architecture, Constance has had a lifelong passion for the arts, spending almost all of her free time acting in plays, singing, and dancing. Neither her architect friends nor the actors she knew could understand how she could be successful at both. "And now I have the one job where all those talents come into play."

After earning her architecture degree, Constance headed for New York City where an architect's job awaited. But after a while, she became disillusioned working in New York, opted for a fresh start, and headed west.

"I always thought that Los Angeles, as a designer, was the place to be because you could do anything you want," Constance says. "I thought, all right, in Los Angeles, you can have one house that looks like a big fish, right next to a house that looks like an English castle. Anything goes, and that really appealed to me."

"The things that are most important to me about the job," Constance says, "are that I see us growing together as a family, as a design team. What I see is that there's such an enormous outpouring of goodwill by everyone. Everyone follows the call of duty and they do it with love. Even if they're dead tired, even if they're cranky, they still do it. I've grown from that."

The schedule, Constance admits, is grueling. "There are challenges every single week. It's impossible. The weather is impossible every single week. There's always something that happens. It's never a picnic. It's never an easy go."

The Team never loses its focus though, and members don't let their personal frustrations sidetrack them. "You watch people react with love," she says. "You know they give of themselves to get it done."

In California, Constance appeared on and won Home and Garden Television's design contest, *Designers' Challenge*. When producers from *Extreme Makeover: Home Edition* began casting for members of a design team, it was love at first sight. Four days after sending in her resume, Constance had the job.

Ten shows into the first season, Constance met J.J. Carrell, the man who had nominated the Walswick family for a makeover. The happy couple was married in May 2005.

"I'm marrying the man of my dreams. I never thought I would find him and I found him on this show. It's amazing," Constance says.

Together with the Walswick family episode, Constance counts the Harris family episode from Season One as one of her personal highlights so far.

"'Sweet' Alice Harris was the very first person on our show who thanked God, who prayed. She just stopped and prayed. She just stopped and she bent her head down. It makes me cry to think about it."

Perhaps it's only natural that Constance would find love on an *EM:HE* site because she believes that building relationships, and not just houses, is what the show is all about.

"I think it's relationships that are created and resolved with design as a basis. And we create relationships with these families that we work with," she says.

At the end of the day, or seven days, all of the hard work pays off in one beautiful moment, Constance says. "What you see in their eyes when they see their houses for the first time, it's an unbelievable feeling. I see a lot of miracles—miracles every single week."

Constance acquired her earliest experience at the side of her architect father. After a few years working as an architect in New York, she headed west and found the perfect opportunity to use her design skill and her acting talent when she landed a spot on the *EM:HE* Design Team. The fact that her dream job led to meeting the man of her dreams is icing on the cake.

Eduardo

A true Renaissance man, Eduardo began his artistic life as a musician, playing piano from the age of 3. By the time he finished grade school, he had mastered woodwinds and percussion, and was one of the only people in the world to play the bass marimba.

When *Extreme Makeover: Home Edition* added Eduardo Xol (pronounced "soul") to the Design Team, they got a lot more than an inspired landscape designer. An award-winning actor, dancer, singer, and musician, the East Los Angeles native has performed with the Los Angeles Philharmonic Orchestra under the direction of Zubin Mehta and the Conservatory of Music in Mexico City.

In his teens, he joined the Mexican Dance Theatre, made his feature film debut in *Zoot Zuit* starring Edward James Olmos, and was asked to join the illustrious Brand Theatre Company after just one audition.

After founding a music and video production company he moved to Mexico City, in 1993 and hit the big time as a singer! As Edi Xol, his first CD, *La Pasion*, yielded two Top 10 videos on the big three Spanish-language networks. He was nominated as video artist of the year alongside Gloria Estefan and Ricky Martin.

Several television roles followed and a few years later he burst onto the U.S. market with the hit single "I'll Be There For You." Several albums and feature films followed, but by 2002 he needed a break. "I needed to step back and reevaluate my career," he says. "I wanted to weigh whether I was in it for the right reasons."

He decided to explore one of his first loves: gardening.

"Whether you're on stage, in front of the camera, or in the garden, the importance of harmony is universal. If you can bring harmony into someone's life by touching an emotional chord through the lyrics of a song or creating an outdoor space for entertaining family and friends, then you should share that gift."

His landscape design work led to an audition for the *Extreme Makeover: Home Edition* cast. It was, he recalls, the opportunity of a lifetime.

His first show—the two-hour Correa-Medeiros episode—was extremely emotional, he remembers.

"I walked through a homeless shelter and I was impacted by what I would be doing in this show. I really was walking into their lives and they were looking for us to help them in some way. That moment was amazing, very powerful."

He has come to know and respect all of his fellow cast members.

"Ty's a very compassionate person," says Eduardo. "And when you are, you can't help but connect with people. This last season for everyone has been really busy. Even when Ty was really tired, he was always really positive and always saying really positive things about everyone."

His favorite moments? "Impossible! There have been so many. The entire experience has been so extraordinary."

No doubt we'll be seeing a lot more of this soulful Renaissance man.

For Eduardo, it's the opportunity to help others that has brought him the greatest joy. "Taking that break mid-career helped teach me to keep my priorities straight, and if those things are in the right place, everything else will follow."

What does the future hold for Eduardo? "I hope to continue to be a member of the show. In terms of the future, I want health and happiness for my family and whatever else comes along is fine. I think what it is in the end is finding a personal balance. What a wonderful place to be. Many other people would love to be in the place I'm in."

Xo

Tugwell FAMILY

I'm impressed

"It's kind of comedic, and yet functional. That's Ty Pennington for you right there."
—Preston

John and Susan Tugwell of Long Beach, California, literally had their lives come crashing down around them when a drunk driver in an SUV plowed through the front door of their home, missing 25-year-old Abbey and her baby by inches. The house was destroyed, and unable to afford to rebuild, the family has been living in a hotel.

The *Extreme Makeover* Team is here to pick up the pieces and put the Tugwell family's life back together.

THE HOUSE

"Good morning, Tugwell family!"

The Team is shocked when it first lays eyes on how extensive the damage is and how close Abbey and the baby were to being killed. Not only did the Tugwells lose their house, precious and irreplaceable memories and heirlooms were also destroyed. A beloved antique armoire was severely damaged.

"This is one of the things we've worked hard emotionally to let go of because it did have some real meaning for us," says Susan Tugwell sadly.

Ty promises the Tugwells they will do everything they can to save their memories.

John and Susan Tugwell meet Ty and the Team.

"We have constant setbacks," admits Alle late in the renovation. "The flooring in the house is still not laid. The tiling is still not done in the master bedroom. The electrical, well, we're having a bit of a problem. The cabinets are not finished. We still need to do the trim. We drew it on paper. Then, it's not what we wanted. It's a mess. It's a mess."

Meanwhile, the Team "stretches" some stiff legs. Bend at the knees!

THE RENOVATION STARTS NOW

While the Tugwells head off to a resort vacation in Las Vegas, the crew sits down to create a design that will feature more space and private areas, plus some ideas for replacing the many cherished items that were lost.

The removal of debris moves quickly, but by the middle of Day 3, the renovation hits a wall. The crew has uncovered evidence of extensive structural damage. Efforts to reinforce the house put the project seriously behind schedule.

By Day 4, however, Paul has completed the difficult work on refurbishing and repairing the armoire. Later, the architect who designs the bathrooms at the Venetian Hotel arrives to help out on Susan's dream bathroom. But the rest of the job is not going nearly as well. On Day 5, concerned that the house will not be ready on time, Alle enlists help from every contractor he can think of, and the crisis is averted.

By the end of Day 6, the pool is finished, and Ty dials 911 for some "expert" help from the fire department to get the pool filled with water. With the family due to arrive in a matter of hours, however, none of the furniture has made it into the house.

"We've never been this far behind before," worries Ty.

It's Day 7, and hundreds of friends and neighbors are gathering to welcome the Tugwells home, but Ty has to make a call to the limousine driver to stall. Lights have to be installed so work can continue into the evening. Frantic workers inside can hear wild cheering as they hurry to install a bathroom counter.

WHAT TIME WAS THAT, AGAIN?

Preston: So, Paul. When do you think we'll get this thing done.

Paul: Shortly.

Preston: Yeah, I don't think so, either.

"Wow!" gushes Susan. "It's more than I would have dreamed of! I know people dream in scales like this, but I don't."

"We might have been a little late," admits Ty, "but in the end, we made some dreams happen."

FIRST NIGHT REVEAL

WELCOME TO YOUR NEW HOME!

It is nearly 11 P.M. when Ty finally announces that the house is finished. The Tugwells—relieved to be out of the limousine—react with shouts of joy and applause when they see their new home for the first time.

The beautiful white exterior with columns moves Susan to tears, which really start to flow when she enters the house and sees the restored armoire.

"This was kindling," she says. "I don't know how you did this."

A new baby grand piano flanks John's restored upright piano. At the other end of the room, a flick of a switch makes the lights go down; blinds cover the windows and a screen lowers to create Cinema Tugwell. The kitchen, with all new stainless steel appliances, sparkles, as does the new master bathroom, with its deep-soak Jacuzzi tub and steam closet shower.

Off the master bedroom, John's former retreat is now a reading room, with bookshelves along one wall. The wall rotates, and Ty has turned the wild chaos of John's storage room into a more manageable space with lots and lots of bins and drawers for keeping the "chaos" under control.

Abbey and Aaron have their own room, as well, which includes a sumptuous and spacious bathroom and an attached baby's room. In the backyard, the old pool has been transformed into an Italian grotto with massive boulders and two waterfalls.

"The best part of the whole thing happened before construction even started," says John Tugwell, "because that's when the sound of the crash was taken out of our heads and replaced by the sound of Ty on the bullhorn."

"There's no way to thank somebody for that," says Susan. "I don't know if the show realizes what they do, really. I get to go home tonight. I get to go home."

"Oh!" says Susan. "Oh my God! Oh, this is so beautiful. This is extraordinary. And there's a fireplace!"

Adds John, "It couldn't be better. It's just that simple. It just couldn't be better."

Whew! And not a minute to spare!

Powell FAMILY

Doctors told single-mother Carrie Powell that her youngest son Keenan, stricken with the rare cell disease mastocytosis, wouldn't live to see his first birthday.

But Keenan proved them all wrong.

The 16-year-old is a high school basketball star with a case full of trophies at home to prove it. Keenan, however, is allergic to impurities in the air. He's been hospitalized more than 20 times—twice in intensive care. His hospital bills have nearly crippled the family.

The problem? The Powell home is infested with mold.

"I love my Mom. Since day one, she worked hard, quit her job, just to get me better, and to see her happiness...it meant everything to me." —Keenan Powell

Carrie Powell and her two sons react with shock and joy when the Team arrives with news that they have been chosen for an extreme makeover. A happy and loving family, it was not always the case. Keenan is lucky to be alive.

THE HOUSE

With Keenan already wheezing, the Powells literally have only a few minutes to take the Team on a tour. In the bathroom ugly swaths of mold stain the walls. Mold infests the ceiling and closet of Keenan's small trophy-filled bedroom. The Powells have tried everything to combat the mold, but it keeps coming back.

"It feels like I'm drowning," Keenan says. His only refuge is the driveway.

Mold is not the only problem. The house is shockingly cramped. Brother Chris sleeps on a tiny couch, as the hallway's strange configuration prevents him from getting a full-sized bed into his room. The kitchen is old and completely inadequate.

While the Powells hand their house keys off to Ty and head for their vacation in New York City, the designers meet in the backyard to talk makeover. Michael proposes a Moroccan villa style for the house, while Alle suggests an addition off the back of the house where a new master bathroom and bedroom will look out onto the garden. Michael also wants to raise the ceiling in the garage to turn it into an indoor basketball court complete with hardwood floors. Ty will take on Keenan's room as his own secret project.

First, the mold problem. Ty calls in experts to analyze the damage. It's worse than they had thought. In fact, it turns out the mold is not merely

fabulo-meter

"So why not go **crazy**? We give her a **full-on Moroccan villa.** Get your **passport**, kids! We're going to **Morocco.**"

—Michael

inconvenient. It's potentially toxic. The renovation is shut down completely until mold experts in hazmat suits sweep the site clean.

It's a full day before construction can begin. Once it does, however, the crew kicks into overdrive. Unfortunately, with 48 hours to go, the sheetrock is only just going up.

The next day, work is still way behind schedule. The backyard looks more like a dirt parking lot than a lush garden. Under a full moon, everybody is working at top speed to get the job done, and by dawn of Day 7, the furniture is going into the house. But with some extra special surprise help from a team of specialists, the makeover is finished on time.

WELCOME TO YOUR NEW HOME!

Carrie Powell breaks into tears when the limousine turns onto the street and she sees the cheering throng of supporters, friends, and well-wishers who have turned out to welcome her and her sons.

"Bus driver!" shouts Ty. "Move that bus!"

When the bus pulls away, Carrie comes face to face with her Moroccan-themed dream house, complete with a towering palm tree in the front yard.

"This is so incredible, it reminds me of my childhood," she says.

Inside, the cramped and haphazardly designed rooms have been opened up and completely transformed into a great room. Carrie, Chris, and Keenan are amazed at their beautiful new furnishings, plush Persian rugs, dazzling state-of-the-art appliances, and their restored antique piano.

In his new room, Chris flops down on the bed and takes in the decor, which includes an authentic barber pole on one wall and a real barber's chair in the corner.

Carrie loves her new room, too. "Oh my God, I'm a goddess," she exclaims as she takes in her new oasis, which includes a massive tiled bathroom with an infinity tub and shower, with water coming out of the ceiling above it.

LOOK WHO DROPPED BY!

Three members of the world-famous Harlem Globetrotters show up to lend a hand. Actually, several very large hands!

In the backyard, Carrie is amazed at her new rock pond, organic garden and her "garden shed," a massive Bedouin-style desert tent. Back in the house, Ty sends Keenan to check out his new bedroom, which he's fitted out with lockers, basketballs, and a small gym.

Keenan is in tears, he is so happy. However, the biggest surprise awaits him in the garage. It's a regulation red-and-blue basketball court, complete with a scoreboard. And who better to break in a new hoop than the hoop masters themselves: the Harlem Globetrotters!

The 'Trotters show Keenan a few of their tricks, and before long, a game of pickup breaks out. Keenan and Chris are in basketball heaven.

"It's a brand new house, a brand new start," says Keenan. He breathes deep and smiles.

"We received a miracle from all of you," says Carrie. "Thank you for helping my son, and thank you for giving us our lives back. I will always be grateful for what you've done for our family."

"Oh my God!" screams Carrie when she sees her new home. "I'm a goddess!"

The Harlem Globetrotters show the boys some tricks in the new garage basketball court.

Brooke Imbriani, a hard-working single-mother of two, didn't hesitate to answer the call when her mother Pam was diagnosed with diabetes. She moved back into her parents' home in San Bernadino, California, to help her ailing mother in any way she could.

"It's what family does," Brooke explained. "When a family member is in need, and you can help, you help."

At the time, the Imbrianis' 1950s-era bungalow wasn't in the greatest shape. It needed lots of repair and could have done with a substantial renovation. The family was starved for space. When her father passed away two years later, the house fell into further disrepair. Brooke had no money and no time to spend on home repair.

Still, Brooke decided there was more she could do to help others.

When Brooke was informed she was a match for someone who needed a bone marrow transplant, she was only too glad to donate. She asked for nothing in return. Not even the recipient's name. She just knew she had to help.

In fact, the recipient was 10-month-old leukemia victim Esmerelda Ramirez. The marrow saved the little girl's life. In an effort to thank this selfless good Samaritan for her literal gift of life, Esmerelda's grateful mother Nancy appealed to *Extreme Makeover: Home Edition*.

"Please find this family," begged Nancy. "I don't know who this family is, but I know you could find this family. Make them a new house just to thank them from the bottom of my heart."

"This was the episode where an enormous number of appliances would not fit through the doorway. We were cutting bathtubs in half and welding them together on the second floor. There was this weirdly shaped staircase that no one had thought out when Michael went shopping for appliances. Sofas and beds and bathtubs had to be demolished and then rebuilt on the second floor. "
—Executive Producer Tom Forman

That's NUTS. AND BOLTS

"Can you guys build a house in five days? From scratch? ...Do you think it's possible, what I'm trying to do? ...I understand. I realize that. Right. So what you're telling me is... no. No? No. That's what I figured you were going to say."
— Ty

THE HOME

"She deserves this makeover," says Ty in their traditional meeting on the bus. "This is a chance to give something back."

From their faces, as they watch this emotional appeal from a grateful mother and her precious daughter, the Team has never been more certain that Brooke Imbriani deserves something extra special.

"Good morning, Imbriani family!" shouts Ty.

Brooke, mother Pam, and Brooke's children, Trevor, 6, and 9-month-old Brooke Lynn, tumble out the front door with excited, awestruck expressions. It turns out the makeover is especially welcome as Brooke's sister Summer, her husband Brett, and their 15-month-old son Tyler are moving in shortly to help share expenses.

The Team happily has arrived just in time!

It is obvious immediately that the house will need more than a makeover. It's way too small for four adults and three children. Worse, it's structurally unsound. The roof has no ridge beam, the walls shake when a door is slammed, and the floors have holes in them.

"This house is literally a disaster waiting to happen," says Ty.

THE RENOVATION BEGINS NOW!

After the Imbrianis head to the airport for their resort vacation in Hawaii, the Team meets to map a strategy. It includes a new kitchen in a 1950s' diner style and a football-themed bedroom for Trevor. A sumptuous new master bedroom for Brooke. A fabulous room where she—for once—can be pampered. For the bleak sun-baked backyard, a pool and a play area for the kids.

Unfortunately, Ty is convinced that nothing short of tearing the entire house down and building from the ground up will work. The Team is flabbergasted. A completely new house in seven days? Impossible!

After dozens and dozens of calls to every home fabrication outfit in the country, Ty finally locates a Canadian contractor who can handle the job.

"We're on our way!"

In no time at all, the house is reduced to rubble and the debris carted away and concrete poured for the new house. It's a tense time as the Team has never attempted anything so ambitious. After a tense day of waiting, the house finally arrives after a long trip from British Columbia. Framing the house together is like assembling a giant puzzle. They are behind schedule.

The Team and crew kick into overdrive. By the end of Day 3, the new swimming pool is in the ground, but something seems to be missing on the house. A crane arrives to lift the roof into place.

Esmerelda and her mother Nancy pay a visit to the site. A couple of familiar faces from the Super Bowl champion New England Patriots drop by for some helpful design tips. There is still a lot to do, however, and the crew works nonstop through the night. Just after dawn the next day, the new house is ready for the Imbrianis' arrival.

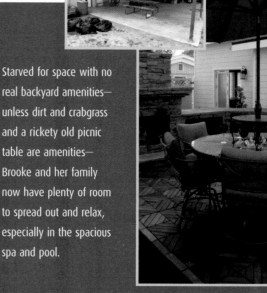

Starved for space with no real backyard amenities—unless dirt and crabgrass and a rickety old picnic table are amenities—Brooke and her family now have plenty of room to spread out and relax, especially in the spacious spa and pool.

WELCOME TO YOUR NEW HOME

Ty welcomes the Imbrianis home as friends and neighbors crowd along the street clapping and cheering.

"Driver! Move that bus!"

Brooke stares in frank, wide-eyed wonder at her new two-storey yellow house with white trim. Pam is delighted with her 1950s' diner-style kitchen, with its checkerboard floor, red appliances, jukebox, old-fashioned soda fountain, and leather booth in one corner. Upstairs, the first stop is a new room for the little ones, complete with a Winnie the Pooh mural. Trevor's football room has fake grass, a stadium mural, and miniature goalposts; Brooke has a new master bedroom with a walk-in closet and sparkling blue-tiled bathroom, and Summer and Brett have a large, beautifully appointed bedroom of their own.

In the backyard, the incredible new pool, hot tub, cabana, and huge patio, complete with an outdoor fireplace, are overshadowed by the presence of Esmerelda and Nancy, who've come to thank Brooke in person.

"Thank you for saving my daughter's life. God bless you, Brooke, you're an angel," says a sobbing Nancy as the two women embrace. "This is my miracle," she says, holding Esmerelda.

"Words can't describe what happened there," says Preston. "It was a divine intervention, not a design intervention this time."

Brooke Imbriani and her extended family react with stunned disbelief to their new home, including the '50s-themed kitchen. Rock 'n roll!

Nancy and daughter Esmerelda arrive to thank Brooke for the greatest gift of all—the gift of life. No words, she says, can express her thanks. Esmerelda was less than a year old when a call went out for bone marrow to save her life. Brooke answered the call. No questions asked. That is what a family does, says Brooke.

Paul DiMeo

Paul says the show has kept his focus sharp about how lucky he is and how much some families struggle. He has come to appreciate their quiet strength and dignity. "These people face adversity every day, and the amazing thing is, they never lose hope. I like to push myself. I think the more we can do for these people, the better, and the better TV show that's made," Paul says.

It's little surprise Paul DiMeo seems so at home on *Extreme Makeover: Home Edition*. The 47-year-old carpenter from Media, Pennsylvania, took part in his first major home renovation at the age of 5.

"The entire household and family had gone to a wedding," he remembers. "Our old oil burner caught fire and the house pretty much burnt to the ground." Later, with reconstruction underway, he recalls, "the contractor went on strike. So my father had to take on the project of rebuilding. The community kind of pulled together to help us out."

And even as a 5-year-old, Paul was chipping in on the site.

"I would do anything I could to help the old man, from carrying paint buckets to whatever. I remember that like it was yesterday."

So Paul has been at this renovation thing for quite some time! In truth, with more than 25 years as a builder, he is the most experienced member of the Extreme Makeover Team. Paul has built sets for theater productions of all sorts; performed hundreds of renovations, ranging from commercial spaces to intricate restorations; and even worked as a roadie for major musical acts from Santana to Bonnie Raitt and Kenny Rogers.

Paul attended Point Park College in Pittsburgh, and it was there, constructing sets for the Pittsburgh Playhouse, that he honed his extraordinary building skills. He also served as stage manager for the American Dance Ensemble. "I built sets. I did over 300 performances of *The Nutcracker*. I'd do pretty much what we do here. I'd load the truck, and we'd move on to the next town."

In the summer of 1980, Paul moved to New York City, where he met Harry Baum and Lynne Michaels, the owners of The Open Space Theater. It would prove to be an extremely important relationship. "These are great people. They always kept me working building their sets."

Paul has made some friends among his cast members, but admits that there are moments. "We're like a family. We have problems sometimes." His favorite sibling? "I certainly have a lot of fun with Preston."

Paul gives a huge amount of credit for the success of the show to Executive Producer Tom Forman. "He's why this is all happening. It's his vision."

Working construction during the day and with The Open Space at night, Paul also freelanced for the Dance Theatre of Harlem, the Yiddish Theater, Carnegie Hall, and numerous Broadway and off-Broadway houses.

"I was swinging a hammer during the day for a construction company, and at night I was doing theater. I was paying my dues." And he was also learning the fine art of dumpster diving, a skill he has put to use on *Extreme Makeover: Home Edition*.

During this period, Paul also recognized that a large part of his talent—and his happiness—lay in helping others. He continually renovated lofts and brownstones in Greenwich Village, Harlem, Tribeca, and the East Village. He was the master carpenter on the restoration of Aaron Burr's landmark brownstone, and has renovated celebrities' homes, including Madonna's.

After 17 years in New York, Paul decided it was time for a change, so he moved to Los Angeles. It didn't take long for his reputation as a fine carpenter to spread, and he soon found himself renovating the homes and businesses of Hollywood's movers and shakers. His client list includes the Beverly Hills Ralph Lauren Polo store, the William Morris Agency, and the homes of Glenn Close, David Niven Jr., Ann Archer, and George Hamilton.

He was the most surprised of all after his audition for *EM:HE*.

"I was the only one in the audition who said, 'This is crazy! How can you build a house in seven days?'" he recalls. "I was very grumpy. They liked that I was very grumpy. They called me and said 'We love you. What are you doing in two weeks?'"

Two seasons later, Paul has earned a reputation as perhaps America's most imaginative bed builder. He's also the team member most likely to be staying up all night on Day 6, pushing himself to get all his projects completed.

Fame, and his newfound security, hasn't changed him.

"The work keeps me real. I'm still a carpenter."

Paul says he has come to love the show largely because he understands what some of these families are going through, and he welcomes the chance to help.

"Up until this show, I was only about two paychecks from being homeless. I think 90 percent of America is that way."

Tracy HUTSON

With her model looks, talent, and warm, charming personality, one might think Tracy Hutson was looking to launch an acting career when she moved to Los Angeles at the age of 21. But although she did some modeling as a teen, the native Texan, who grew up in Austin and the Dallas area, wasn't looking for a career in the entertainment industry.

Modeling and acting jobs helped pay the rent while she pursued her real love—interior design.

"I never really focused on acting at all," says Tracy, who has appeared in several films, commercials, TV sitcoms, and theater productions. "I never really wanted to be an actress. I always wanted to be an interior designer, so acting supplemented my income until I got my business off the ground."

That business was Tracy Hutson Designs, the company she launched in 1999. An impressed client heard that *Extreme Makeover: Home Edition* was scouting design talent and thought that Tracy would be a perfect fit.

The show's producers agreed.

Responsible for shopping and style on *EM:HE,* Tracy admits to being a serious shopper in both her personal life and in her design work as well. And, as she demonstrates regularly on the show, she's more likely to be found in a thrift shop or antique store than in a Beverly Hills boutique.

When she's not working or shopping, Tracy might just be...sleeping. "I love going to the beach, spending time outside, spending time with my friends, just relaxing," she says. "But sleeping is definitely something I like to do every chance I get. We don't get much sleep on the show."

Of all the episodes that she has taken part in, Tracy singles out the Vardon family as being a particularly special one.

"I love finding bargains. My style is very eclectic. I love going to flea markets, I love having things made...sort of like finding the diamond in the rough."

As for rough, Tracy is no pushover with a hammer!

"We're just this big family," Tracy says of her Design Team family.

"Ty is such a goofball and it's just this loving, sort of dysfunctional family. We're always picking on each other and playing pranks. Every day is funny. We can always find the humor in any situation."

Even though she lists "sleeping" as a favorite activity, Tracy has lots of plans. There's a new baby on the way, a much-awaited return to the show, and soon the launch of her own line of children's and baby furniture!

"Those boys—just the courage of Stefan, to nominate his family, and the fact that this 14-year-old has so much on his plate, having to be the interpreter. It was incredible. He was just such a beautiful young man. It was just such a great thing to be a part of. He ended up getting a scholarship for college."

The youngest Vardon son, 12-year-old Lance, who is blind and autistic, provided Tracy with her most memorable moment on the show.

"There was just this beautiful, magical moment in the middle of all this chaos, with us revealing their new house. I mean you've never seen a smile so big. It was just a great, great episode."

Tracy has spent the latter part of Season Two on maternity leave as she and husband Barry Watson of *7th Heaven* fame prepared to write a new chapter in their personal lives.

Having recently moved into a new, larger three-bedroom home near Los Angeles in anticipation of their own newest addition, Tracy laughs off any suggestion the couple will be undertaking any remodeling adventures of their own any time soon.

"I have my hands full already. Thanks very much!"

Walswick FAMILY

The Carrell and Walswick families became great friends under the absolute worst circumstances. The two families met at a clinic, where J.J. Carrell's wife, Kelley, and Martha Walswick's husband, Greg, were both being treated for brain tumors. Sadly, Kelly died. Not too long after, Greg died, too.

Kelley Carrell's last selfless wish to J.J. was that he remodel Martha's kitchen.

Even when Greg was alive, the Walswick home was a tight fit for nine kids. But during Greg's three-year battle with cancer, the house fell into complete disrepair. With two children in college and seven more between the ages of 4 and 17, Martha had all she could handle—and then some.

J.J. had an inspiration. What better way, he realized, to fulfill his wife's final wish for their good friends, the Walswicks, than a complete *Extreme Makeover: Home Edition* remodel? J.J. knew Kelley would approve. It would honor both her and Greg. Even better, he knew Martha really needed—and deserved—some good news.

Good news is definitely on the way.

THE HOUSE

Hundreds of neighbors and friends are waiting on the street as the *EM:HE* bus pulls up in front of the Walswick home in Loma Linda, California.

"Good morning, Walswick family!" bellows Ty through his bullhorn.

The street erupts in wild and cheering pandemonium as the surprised family reacts with screams and shouts of joy and disbelief.

The house tour is emotional, especially when the kids cluster around an old green rocking chair. Martha explains that when the children were babies, Greg would sit for hours rocking them to sleep.

"You could feel the love," says Paige. "You could feel that Greg was there, watching over his entire family."

Ty rallies the Walswicks with his bullhorn wakeup call.

"These kids really miss their dad. He had dreams of building this house and renovating it for his family, and he never got a chance to do that. So we're going to do it for him in his honor."

It's no surprise that with so many kids, space is at a premium. One of the boys' bedrooms is a hallway their sisters have to walk through to get to their own room.

All four girls share one room. The older sisters, Maureen and Emily, crave more privacy. Martha's room, piled floor-to-ceiling with boxes, looks more like a storage room than a master bedroom. In the bathroom, Martha explains that the tile flooring was the last project she and Greg did together

"These kids really miss their dad," says Ty. "He had dreams of building this house and renovating it for his family, and he never got a chance to do that. So...we're going to do it for him, and we're going to do it for him in his honor."

As Ty wishes the Walswicks well on their resort spa vacation in Palm Springs, the Team meets to plan the makeover. The object? Space!

An addition off the back of the house will give Philip and Gregory a real bedroom, which Ty volunteers to take on as his personal secret project. Michael will build the ultimate kitchen for Martha. Emily and Maureen need their own rooms. The Team designs a sunroom for the back of the house that will double as a game room.

THE RENOVATION BEGINS NOW!

On D-day, Contractor John Coleman reminds his crew what it's all about. "They won't know who you are, they won't know your faces, but every time they walk through that door, they'll know your heart."

By Day 3, the framing is completed and sheetrock covers almost every other wall in the house. The renovation is running ahead of schedule. Dawson, however, is "stumped" on his tree house project for the backyard. Did someone say "stump?!" Ty has found some creative contractors who have the perfect solution.

A new house will be a new beginning, but important mementos, like Greg's favorite rocking chair, will be preserved. Paige comes up with a novel idea—a treasure box. She asks everyone to write a short letter to the family.

"We'll put all those letters inside the treasure box and present them to the family when they get home. This is going to be a treasure box full of love."

Meanwhile, Constance enlists a group of neighborhood girls to pose for the ballerina silhouettes she will appliqué to the walls in Katherine and Bridget's room.

With 48 hours to go, the windows are installed and the interior is ready to be painted. To help reupholster Greg's rocking chair, Martha's sewing club is hard at work on new slipcovers. An oak tree Dawson has ordered as a "memory tree" for Greg also arrives.

On the evening of Day 6, Paige strolls outside, and is moved to tears. A crowd of friends is holding candles as a show of support. Hours from dawn, hungry and exhausted, the Team is surprised when neighbors appear with home-cooked lasagna and a huge cake.

"It kind of boosted spirits for that night," says Paige, "and kept us going to the wee hours of the morning."

With the family only hours from returning, Dawson installs an engraved redwood plaque at the base of the memory tree. The renovation is finished.

The Team celebrates silently with an impromptu candle-lighting ceremony in front of the "Family Tree of Light."

WELCOME TO YOUR NEW HOME!

Thousands of excited friends and neighbors and well-wishers have gathered to await the Walswicks' return. As their limo turns the corner for home, the family collectively gasps as they glimpse the cheering crowd lining their street.

"Driver! Move that bus!"

A beautiful white picket fence frames a beautiful new home. Martha and the kids are staggered.

Moments later their screams of joy taper to reverent silence and tears when they come upon Greg's memory tree and its engraved inscription.

It's as if the front door opens not only into a new home, but to new hope.

Everything has been opened up. The new kitchen, featuring an

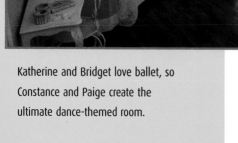

Katherine and Bridget love ballet, so Constance and Paige create the ultimate dance-themed room.

The two designers demonstrate the perfect form for the ballet barre. Or are they showing Ty and the guys how to kick a field goal?

fabulo-meter

"We're going **glam rock** on that side, and **flower power** on that side. Really **groovy**. I kind of want to make it a little, you know, *edgy*."
—Michael

Michael is firing on all cylinders with these knock-out concepts for Emily and Maureen's new bedrooms. Kind of Haight-Ashbury meets ultra-hip Lion Country Safari.

What happens if the girls need some private time? No problem. Slide close the opaque glass door and it's two separate bedrooms.

"We got a hot mix, **quarter**-slab, **half**-slab. We got the **pavers** inside there. We have the **C.E.T.** ready-mix in there. We got a **sheer** wall, the **pony wall**, the **stones** up. Everything else is pretty much **F.D.A**-approved. We've got a **mole** in the **hole**, a pony in the **chute**. We've got gravy in the **biscuit**, and we are ready for **departure**. Can you **communicate** that to your **mom?** Oh, by the way, **don't forget** to tell her she's going to **love** the **zebra** print."

—Ty has some fun on a joke phone call with little Bridget and Caroline Walswick

eight-burner stove and three ovens, is a cook's dream. The living room is welcoming and spacious. In their new bedrooms, Maureen and Emily finally have the privacy they lacked. The dividing wall is an opaque glass partition that can be opened or closed as they wish! Eric is thrilled with his room, which even includes furniture constructed from cardboard. Katherine and Bridget are "tickled pink" with their ballerina room.

Maureen will be delighted with a new more spacious bedroom, which features a new bed she can actually sleep in and will no longer double as storage space for all the boxes of…whatever. What the heck was all that stuff anyway?

The kids love the rope-swing their dad built out back. Dawson figures it will be cool to build the ultimate tree house—so over the top it will make the Swiss Family Robinson tree house look like a pup tent.

It's a beautiful new day when the family sees its new home for the first time. A new day and hope for many wonderful new beginnings.

It's all so hard to take in, but Martha knows Greg would be proud.

Martha's new bedroom is bright and beautiful. Her bathroom, with a deep-soak tub and huge tiled shower, also has four of the old bathroom tiles in the middle of the floor.

In the new addition, Ty has done up Gregory and Philip's room with a snowboard-themed side for Gregory, and an outdoor look on Philip's side, complete with a birch tree, a map wall, and a rock-climbing wall.

Outside, the back porch area is beautifully appointed with state-of-the-art grill and patio furniture. The solarium/game room inspires hoots of joy from the kids, but it is Greg's reupholstered rocker in the corner that moves them.

"They wanted to keep that chair," says Martha. "And to see it in the game room, and to think that this is going to be in here when the kids are in there playing is really wonderful."

The backyard is dominated by a huge tree house which functions also as an outdoor theater. Its elaborate stage features a large projection screen that will allow the Walswicks and their guests to watch their favorite movies outdoors under the stars.

"You get a feeling of joy," says Emily Walswick, "because this is a place where my family can be together and really feel like a family."

"It'll be really great to have those memories in our hearts and in our home."

A special feature of the new home is a memory wall.

"There are 11 places where candles go,"explains Ty. "An 11th spot for Greg. They can light a candle in his honor and embrace their new beginning. It's about showing what this whole project was about, and that's the family. Mom...Dad."

Cadigan-Scott
FAMILY

When Diane Cadigan-Scott died suddenly, her eight children and grieving husband wondered how they would survive. But none of the children could have been prepared for the cruel blow that followed. Sixteen days later, father Mark died suddenly, also.

Reeling from the losses, eldest sisters Jennifer, 23, and Janice, 21, their five sisters —Theresa, Dolly, Rachel, Kelli, Jackie—and brother, Danny, suddenly were entirely on their own. Jennifer and Janice moved home to take care of the family. If they hadn't, the kids likely would have been split up in the foster care system. They could not let that happen. After losing both parents so suddenly and so tragically, they had only one thing in mind: Keep the family together.

It is hard to imagine anything worse than losing both parents unexpectedly within the span of two weeks.

"They've had the worst year of their lives," says Ty. "But in seven days we're going to give them a clean start."

It wouldn't be easy. The house was not huge. Even under the best of circumstances, eight kids can really wear a house out. With both parents gone, however, and bills and payments piling up and up, well, Janice and Jennifer realized they needed some help.

"I just want to let you know how much it would mean to me to see my family have a nice home where we could all live together," says an emotional Jennifer.

"Step on it bus driver!" shouts Michael. The Team, already on the bus headed to the Cadigan-Scott home in Livermore, California, cheers and claps enthusiastically.

They can feel in their hearts that this extreme makeover experience will be something special.

THE HOUSE

"Good morning, Cadigan-Scott family!"

Ty's bullhorn wake-up call draws the screaming, squealing Cadigan-Scott girls out of the house in a raucous, hopping, hugging, cheering jumble. The joyous shrieking is deafening—almost painful! Teenager Danny Cadigan-Scott shakes his head. Paul and Ty flash Danny sympathetic smiles.

"Dude, we feel your pain!"

The first room they visit is their parents' bedroom, virtually untouched since their passing some 10 months before. Every square inch of its walls is covered with children's artwork and other family mementos.

"All of this, every piece of this, needs to go in a scrapbook," says Michael.

Janice and Jennifer admit the need to move on. All they ask is that their mother's favorite armoire be saved.

The kitchen is falling apart. Cabinets hang on single hinges. The dining room is a mess of mismatched furniture, including two beds where Jennifer and Jackie, 16, sleep. Kelli, 20, and Rachael, 18, share a bedroom with old bunk beds. Dolly and Theresa share a room, too. Janice and Danny, 20, a budding

"Before the extreme makeover," says Janice, "we had a house that was literally in shambles and barely livable. Now we have a place to go where we can call home. It has meant the world to us, and we know that our parents are looking down on it saying, 'Thank you.' We can all sit down and have dinner as a family."

Design 101

Tracy: They need fresh. Hip. Cool. Fun.

"I don't think we could live without the heated toilet seats. There's just something about going to the bathroom at 3 A.M. and really waking up to that surprisingly cold toilet seat," Janice says with a grin.

guitarist, have jerry-rigged rooms in a converted workshop off the garage.

Amazingly, all eight share a single, tiny bathroom.

The backyard is empty and overgrown, but huge. There is a lot of room in it for a large addition and whatever else the designers can dream up. After he and Paul stumble across some of golf-mad Mark Cadigan's old clubs, Preston proposes building a golf green or miniature golf course in the yard.

"You could feel the sadness in the house," says Preston, "because it was left as it was when the tragedy occurred."

"This family needs a lot of things," says Ty. "They obviously need a new house, but they also need a lot of healing. From what I could tell by looking in their eyes, the one thing they really want from us is change."

It's time to get started. While Ty ushers the kids into their stretch limousine for their week-long vacation, the Design Team sits down to plan the makeover. All are in agreement that what the kids need is space. Lots and lots of new space. A renovation that spells fresh and fun, and is full of new hope.

Once they have all signed off on the plan, demolition begins.

"Say 'farewell' to this rather innocuous-looking post-war structure," says Preston as the house comes down around him, "and say 'hello' to a really inventive looking, modernist home."

For a special touch, Preston selects a pair of giant redwood trees he will plant in honor of Diane and Mark. Later, Ty lightens the mood by making a prank telephone call to the family. Schoolteacher Jennifer will be getting a new bedroom with a "pre-school" theme. Danny's room, meanwhile, will be entirely done in leopard print pattern. And Ty jokes that the Team thought it would be great for Rachael, Jackie, Dolly, and Theresa if they all shared a room.

"Ty, I'm moving in with you if you do that," says Dolly.

By the morning of Day 4, the house is starting to take shape, although it still lacks a roof. Soon though, it becomes apparent the ambitious extension and backyard pool have pushed the project over budget.

To raise money, the Team decides to organize a benefit concert. "It was fun," says Preston. "It wasn't good, but it was fun." More importantly, it raised enough money to

ABOVE AND BEYOND

The renovation has gone way over budget. But the Team insists on going all the way with the renovation they promised these kids. Michael comes up the inspired idea of throwing a benefit concert in a park.

"That's a good idea!" says Preston.

"We'll go," volunteers Paul.

"You have to go," jokes Michael. **"You guys are performing."**

finish the house. Tracy and Michael soon head off to San Francisco to complete their shopping with a bag of cash on the front seat of their car.

It's controlled chaos as the Team unloads furniture. With the Cadigan-Scotts due back in a matter of hours, the last major item goes up in the new entranceway: a skylight featuring two doves symbolic of Diane and Mark.

More than 3,000 well-wishers greet the family on its return home. And what a home it is. The Cadigan-Scott girls—unable to contain their surprise and delight—set an *EM:HE* decibel level record for Loudest Screaming.

"It is the coolest-looking house I've ever seen," says Janice. "It's one of a kind; it's beautiful," Jennifer says.

Inside, the screaming erupts again when the girls see the new living room with light-colored hardwood floors, opulent furnishings, and state-of-the-art electronics and appliances—including nine separate television monitors with nine individual headsets and remote controls. In the new kitchen, the sparkling stainless steel refrigerator is filled with a year's supply of pizza.

Equipped with maps Constance has drawn up to help them navigate their new—humongously spacious—home, the Cadigan-Scotts tear off to discover their own rooms. Kelli's room is a gothic castle, complete with faux torches, gargoyles, and a stone wall; Jackie's firefighter room has brick walls, hoses, and a bed made out of steel ladders. Rachael's room has a combination Hawaiian, leopard-print theme. Dolly and Theresa share a new, beautifully detailed and much bigger room. Janice's room is simple but classy,

with abstract art and an array of colors; Jennifer's room has the sophisticated look she always dreamed of, and includes her mother's newly restored armoire.

The seven girls go ballistic with delight when they discover the new bathroom: seven sinks, seven mirrors, a huge Jacuzzi tub, two showers, and two toilets!

Danny finally gets to see the room Ty has set up for him: a music room, with guitars and rock posters on the walls, and a wall-sized amplifier with 12-inch speakers in it. He also gets his own rock 'n roll bathroom, decorated in black and chrome.

The family is moved to silent tears when the Team reveals the new skylight with symbolic "two doves" and the memory wall.

"Our parents are never going to leave us," says Janice. "For us to see two doves when we walk in and two trees when we walk out, it's a good reminder. You know they're looking down on us."

"It's unbelievable," says Kelli. "It's like a dream come true. It's like a fairy tale."

"I love my sisters," says Danny. "I love all seven of them. This house will change our future so much."

"I know that my parents are so happy right now that we can all stay together and continue living together," says Janice.

"When we first laid eyes on our new home we were thinking that there is no way this is the same house we left only seven days before. It looks like a retro model home. We were all thinking 'This is our house?' It is still hard to believe this house was built —and not only built but designed—for us!" —Janice

"The extreme makeover gave us a new beginning. One that we never could have achieved by ourselves. It not only gave us a new beginning, but it also ensured that we could all stay together in the same house. It was a huge relief for everyone, but especially the youngest. It ensured they would not have to leave the house they grew up in and they would not end up in, foster homes or split up amongst family." —Janice

Garay FAMILY

Johnny and Veronica Garay and their family react with joy when the Team arrives.

Ty has informed the crew that this is no ordinary makeover.

"We are blessed with working for a wonderful family here. Johnny counsels children who are at risk."

"I'm not gonna sit here and cry and whine and feel bad about what's going on in my community," says Johnny. "I'm out here trying to put a stop to the violence, to inform, re-educate the minds of our youth."

Johnny and Veronica Garay felt pushed to the limit raising their four young children when a sudden tragedy struck and nearly pushed them over the edge.

Johnny's mother had come for a visit. In the middle of the night, there was a gang shootout on the street outside the Garay's home, which is not a completely unfamiliar occurrence in this section of south-central Los Angeles. However, this act of random violence would change Johnny Garay forever. A stray bullet ripped through their living room window and struck Mother Garay in the head as she slept on the couch.

She was killed instantly. For Johnny, it was a cruel and bitter irony. Johnny Garay counsels children and young people on the dangers of gangs. His whole life has been dedicated to helping people free themselves from the dead-end of gangs and gang violence.

At the time of the shooting, Johnny's mother had five young children of her own, ranging from 5 months to 9 years old. With her gone, there was strong risk they would be separated and put into foster care. But Johnny and Veronica Garay would not let this happen and volunteered to take in all of Johnny's siblings. Overnight they were faced with the enormous responsibility of raising nine kids.

"What you see on TV is about 14 minutes of Ty showing the family their home. But usually we shoot about four hours or more of tape. We had Garay kids everywhere. This was the episode where everyone on the crew was a babysitter."

—Executive Producer Tom Forman

Sadly, one of the Garay's children, David, is a nonverbal autistic special-needs child. Desperate for more space, Johnny moved the entire family into the biggest house he could afford—a 100-year-old fixer-upper that was falling apart. For Johnny and Veronica, their problems had just begun. Social services demanded repairs be made immediately. If not, the children would be removed from the house and installed in foster care. Johnny couldn't afford to make the repairs. But no way could he allow social services to take his kids away.

Johnny has spent his whole life fighting for families. He could not give up fighting for his own. But, he admits, he could really use some reinforcements.

THE HOUSE

When the Team bus rolls up to the Garay house, it's obvious just how dire the family's needs are. Anxious to get started, Ty rallies the family with his infamous wake-up call.

"Good morning, Garay family!"

One after another the Garays tumble out the front door in a whooping, clapping, hopping, cheering frenzy. They meet the Team, and Johnny takes them on a tour. The Team is in shock. The house is in horrible condition. There are so many holes the walls resemble Swiss cheese. Creeping webs of mold stain the ceiling. They cannot believe it when Johnny insists all 11 of them share a single bathroom!

Johnny and Veronica have no door on their bedroom. When they need some privacy, he borrows the shower rod and curtain and hoists it into the doorjamb. Unfortunately, the worst room is David's. It's small and cramped and cheerless, and the walls list dangerously.

Ty wonders if the house is livable. Quite literally it appears that the entire structure could topple with the slightest nudge. First things first: it's time Johnny and his family had some good news. The family is headed to a well-deserved vacation at Disneyland!

The excited family learns where it will spend a dream vacation.

"This is our first time taking a vacation together as a family," says Johnny.

Then it's straight to work for the Team.

"These children have been through so much," says Michael. "But now we've been given an opportunity to give these kids a future."

How's that Again?

"It's not a **real** dinosaur. It's like a **paulosaurus.**
Then over **here,** we have the **bunkosaurus.**" —Paul

"**Dinosaurs** don't **frighten** kids.
Dirty **socks** frighten kids." —Ty

THE RENOVATION BEGINS NOW!

Sitting down to noodle out a game plan, the Team overwhelming agrees that the notion of renovation is out of the question. The house will be demolished. They will have to start from scratch.

The lot is of fair size. But for the room they need to accommodate 11, there is only one option. Up. And up. The Team itself wonders if it is crazy proposing a three-storey house from scratch in seven days.

Before breaking ground on the renovation, however, Constance researches autism to better accommodate David's needs. She speaks with two consultants from Step by Step, a company that helps people understand kids with disabilities. Consistency and trust, the consultants explain, are hugely important issues for autistic kids. They suggest the Team create a book to send to David with pictures of what his room will look like before he even steps into his new room. That should help ease his anxiety about the new surroundings.

On his tour, Johnny informed the Team how important his Mexican heritage was to him and his family. He would love a home that both reminds his kids of where they came from and provides hope and inspiration for the future. They love music. Johnny routinely borrows instruments from his local church so he and his family can play traditional music together.

Ty lights up with an idea! He lets the Team know that the third floor will be his special project: a loft for music, study, and family time will take up the entire third floor of the house!

The Team understood that heritage was very important to Johnny Garay and his family, and incorporated the family's Mexican ancestry into this elegant new dining room and living room. "It's beautiful," says Veronica.

"I couldn't understand all the emotions that were going through me," admits Veronica. "This is a new house. This is *our* new home. My kitchen." She sighed dreamily. "I don't have to cook on a two-burner stove anymore!"

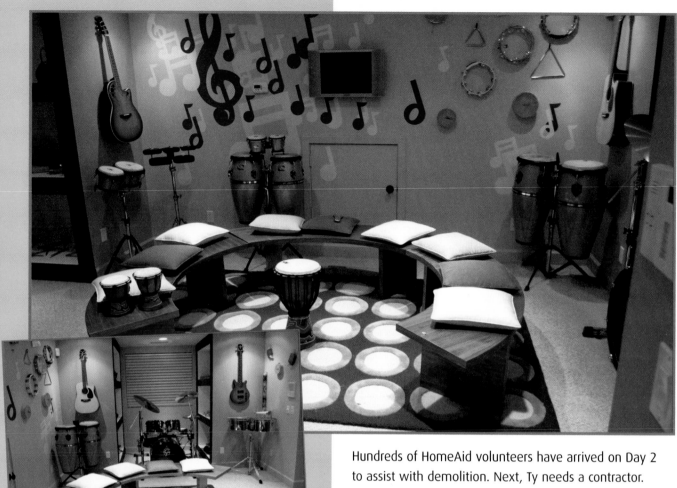

Johnny believes that part of being a family is sharing your heritage. A huge part of their Mexican heritage is music. The family loves music, and loves playing music together...so much so that he often borrows instruments from the local church. Now they have everything they need to make beautiful music—together.

"I think we have outdone ourselves," concludes Ty. "It was the biggest house we've done, some of the biggest rooms we've done, for one of the best families we've ever worked for."

Hundreds of HomeAid volunteers have arrived on Day 2 to assist with demolition. Next, Ty needs a contractor. HomeAid Chairman Jeff Slavin arrives with two men in dark suits, Peter Shea and Bert Selva of Shea Homes, one of the largest construction companies in the world.

"They built the Golden Gate Bridge. They built the Hoover Dam," explains Ty. "I'm thinking they're going to be able to build this house."

But time is short. Only six days until the Garays return home! Shea and Selva call in an army of builders from across the country. Miraculously, the frame for a brand new three-storey house is erected in less than 32 hours! By the day's end, the house is complete. Its size is shocking—even to the Team that designed it. It seems to go on endlessly, room after room after room, with huge dining and common areas, an enormous kitchen, and several bathrooms.

But there are still many finishing touches to be added to the inside. With less than 24 hours to go, the Team is cleared to start moving in the furniture. Johnny and Veronica have requested that a Native Mexican priestess bless the house before their return. A priestess is invited to perform a blessing on the house. And now the Garays' new home is ready!

WELCOME TO YOUR NEW HOME!

The limousine rolls up the street and the excited family leans into the windows to catch glimpses of the hundreds of friends and neighbors waving and cheering from the street.

"Driver!" bellows Ty through his bullhorn. "Move that bus!"

Johnny Garay climbs out first, blinks a few times, then puts his hand to his face in tearful disbelief. "I feel like I'm having a dream! It's...unbelievable."

The Garays erupt in joy as they get their first look at their new home. The rickety house that was nearly falling down has become a three-storey mansion built by one of America's finest homebuilders.

With nine children to contend with, Veronica needs all the help she can get. Her huge new kitchen and utility room include two heavy-duty washing machines, two dryers, and two Titanic-sized refrigerators, and a large dishwasher. Their new master suite has all the luxuries Johnny and Veronica could ever have dreamed of—including a large private bath with hot tub!

Ty leads the family upstairs for the reveal of his special project: a brand new fully equipped music room!

For the kids, the Team created more private spaces suited to their unique and individual interests. Christina wants to be a spy. So now she has her own spy-theme bedroom. Iris loves to play dress-up. Her room features a platform stage and a closet full of clothes and costume jewelry. "Every time she enters her room," says Constance, "she's a winner." The three younger boys are big dinosaur fans. Their new room makes Jurassic Park look like a chicken coop!

Tailoring each room to each child's need was not easy. But they all seemed pleased. But the biggest test was yet to come. What would David think of his room?

His smile said it all.

"I think this might be the most deserving family I've ever met," explains Ty.

"Johnny went through a horrible ordeal, is raising his own kids and his mother's, and, at the same, is helping out a community. He never really has a moment for himself. He gives his whole life to other people. I think that qualifies him as one of the most deserving people."

Friends Helping Friends

EM: Home Edition Live! in New York City!
Fuhgedaboudit!

Yo! Petey! Joey! 'Zup?
NYC Firefighters Pete Wasserman and Joe Liselli—
"hanging out" at their Hell's Kitchen apartment—
get the surprise of a lifetime! The Extreme Team
has a short 12 hours to completely renovate
their tiny apartment—live on network television!

The two September 11 veterans greet the Team
on the sidewalk. Since these guys put their lives on
the line every day, the Team is putting it all on the
line to help them out. Just to say, "Thanks."

On September 11, 2001, Pete and Joe woke up and raced to their fire houses for duty. It was only then that Joe learned 15 of his buddies at the firehouse had been killed in the explosion. But the two pushed that all aside and did their job. For two months and nearly 18 hours a day, they dug through the rubble, pulling out bodies of the fallen. No surprise they had no time to fix up their apartment.

Ty tells them not to worry, and sends them both off to a much-deserved fishing vacation in Key West, Florida.

The Team has 12 hours!

"In many ways this was the toughest thing we've ever done. Because as we learned, it can't be done. Renovating a house in seven days is crazy; renovating an entire apartment in a day is...stupid."
—Executive Producer Tom Forman

Michael directs traffic, workers scramble to remove junk and debris, and others just as quickly haul in new furniture and fixtures. It's complete chaos! The clock is probably the last thing they need to remind them how short of time they are.

Joe and Pete were both born in Long Island and were friends in college. After September 11, the apartment became a crash pad for a lot of their exhausted firefighter colleagues. Joe's girlfriend, Suzy, said she was so terrified of the mess she was afraid to even step inside!

We basically shut down Eighth Avenue and turned it into a television studio.
—Executive Producer Tom Forman

"Ty was the most impressed with how cool the apartment was. So he's rushing the guys through the reveal trying to explain every cool feature but he's got—like—only 10 minutes. And he just ran out of time. It was the weirdest ending to a live show in the history of television."

—Executive Producer Tom Forman

It's late—and the Team is freaking out from stress—when popular morning show host Regis Philbin arrives to lend some support. Just in time, as Ty needs him to make a few calls for some Big Time reinforcements.

As unbelievable as it sounds, in only 12 hours the Team and crew have torn down walls, ripped out electrical wiring and cabinets, put in new fixtures and rewired, installed all new plumbing, put up new walls, laid down carpet—and even installed a deluxe espresso machine!

Thanks to Joe and Pete. And especially to the brave police and firefighters who didn't make it. God bless.

Wofford FAMILY

In 2000, the Wofford family suffered a devastating loss. Teresa Wofford entered the hospital with flu-like symptoms. Shockingly, at age 41, she died.

Brian Wofford was devastated. An operator of a small chiropractic office, he is not a rich man. Unless, as his many friends and neighbors have come to understand and appreciate, a man's riches are measured in his generosity and devotion. He gets up at 4:30 every morning and ends his workday around 11 every night. And he still finds time to coach basketball.

The Wofford kids miss their mother. Each of them—especially eldest daughter Becca—has made countless sacrifices to help keep the family together because that is what Teresa would have wanted. But it hasn't been easy. Brian has refinanced their three-bedroom home three times already. He had to sell the precious wedding ring he scrimped six years to buy his beloved wife.

It's a huge outpouring—literally—when the Woffords learn they have been chosen for a home makeover. As Brian and his eight kids rush outside to meet the Team, the joy is tinged with sorrow by the memory of Teresa Wofford, Brian's wife.

Brian never asks for anything for himself, says a family friend. His theory is, she says, there's always someone else who needs it more.

"Let's give Brian and his family the best house they can imagine," Ty tells the Team. The agreement is unanimous.

THE HOUSE

"Good morning, Wofford family!"

After a spirited series of introductions and an intense pickup game of basketball, the Team takes a tour of the house. They all have the same question: How in the world do nine people fit in this house?

How do you fit nine people into three bedrooms?

Brian smiles. You be creative. The four boys sleep in one room in the garage and the girls double up in rooms in the house. Brian's bedroom also serves as his office, which is basically a fold-down table that he sets up when it's time to work.

The kitchen is small and run-down. Cupboard doors hang off their hinges and the stove is falling apart. There is no real dining area where the entire family can gather for meals. All nine share a single bathroom.

On another level, the Team uncovers serious structural problems with the home as well. There are two serious leaks in the roof, some foundation problems, and the fences around the property are rotting.

As Ty sends the Woffords on a week-long vacation on St. Thomas in the U.S. Virgin Islands, the Team gets busy laying out a design to help this family heal.

Ty: When was the last time you built a house?

Contractor Bill: Actually, we've never built a house.

Ty: Never built a house?

Bill: Not once in 22 years.

Ty: OY. So...you've never built a house in six days, either?

Bill: No.

"Brian's like the most unselfish human on the planet," says Ty. "He doesn't care anything about his own needs. He just wants a bigger house for this family and his kids. He just wants them to be happy."

For a family that loves playing together, the new home will feature an entire floor devoted to sports. Plus a little something special for Brian.

Design 101

Michael: Can we merge, somehow, aliens and lions?

Preston: A spaceship that crashed in the Serengeti?

With eight kids and one adult, the Team had to do a lot of homework when it came to designing a new room for each one of them—especially as each seemed to have a completely unique personality. Anna is into horses, so she will get the cowgirl treatment. Esther loves monkeys. Maybe a jungle theme. Lizzie loves to shop. Her room will be a boutique. Elijah and Aaron like aliens and lions. Hmmmm. Luke is a handyman. His room may be a kind of...well...you get the idea.

Paul: The little green men come out of the spaceship, climb up the ladder. You're in the spaceship. That's where they sleep.

Ty: Paul, what's happening?
Paul: In this room, my friend? Well, we got lions over here. We got aliens over here. This is the spaceship bed.

THE RENOVATION BEGINS NOW!

The decision is it will not be a complete demolition, but pretty close. Except for two walls in the garage, the house will be torn down and rebuilt. As befitting the Southern California location, the Team settles on a classic coastal design for the exterior, with an interior focus on maximum space. It will feature common rooms on the main floor, a spacious kitchen, living room, and dining area. Paul volunteers to build them a table with a top that looks like a basketball court.

Most of the kids will have their own bedrooms. For Becca, who has assumed so much of the mothering role in the family, the design team will provide a resort-like room that will serve as her own personal retreat. Lizzie likes to shop, so she will have a room that is set up like a boutique. For the younger kids, the team will come up with funky ways to combine themes for double rooms. But one thing's for sure. No bunkbeds!

Luke is a budding handyman, so naturally, Ty takes a special interest in his room. It will be Ty's secret project. He will fill it with tools and let Luke finish the room as he wants.

Brian Wofford will have a striking master suite, with an office, bedroom, and large bathroom. The centerpiece of the design will be an indoor gymnasium, two storeys high, with workout equipment and a basketball court!

Outdoors, the Team will install a huge hot tub for the entire family to enjoy. In all, they have laid out a mammoth 4,600-square-foot house, one of the largest projects the Team has ever taken on. And to make it even more daunting, Ty selects a contractor who has never built a house!

That contractor is Bill Larson, head of Pacific Commercial Construction. Bill's been in the business for 22 years, but his projects have always been banks, malls, and other commercial properties. He's never built a house period, never mind building one in six days. But he is a friend of Brian Wofford, he's a professional, and he wants to help.

By the end of Day 2, the house is demolished. By sundown of Day 3, the roof is on the new home!

Paul is overrun with projects. He enlists Lizzie and Becca's high school girls' basketball team to help him with one of the most important jobs: refinishing the rolltop desk that was Teresa's favorite piece of furniture. It will go in Brian's office. By the end of Day 6, the house is ready for furniture.

The Team is blown away by Bill's skill. This has been one of the fastest renovations ever. Finished early, the Team challenges Becca's basketball team to a little game. The Team is destroyed.

Monkeying Around

When the Team finds itself dangerously behind schedule, they call in some reinforcements, including Cody, the Master Designer.

Here, Cody drills Preston and Paul in sure-fire techniques to use when Ty bugs them with questions like, "How we doin'?" or "Aren't you done yet?"

Later Cody puts in a call to the family in St. Thomas to update them on the renovation.

A Perfect 10?

Michael steps up to the line for the critical "cake toss" in the First Annual *Extreme Makeover: Home Edition* "Design Team" Olympics. Either that or he has spotted Ty with his famous bullhorn and has taken matters into his own hands.

Paul DiMeo is ready for anything—including high tide or torrential rain—as he strolls on site dressed in a wet suit and flippers.

It can get so hectic building a new house in seven days, it can seem like...well...a zoo, as Preston and Tracy discover. Meanwhile, Ty has a close encounter with a boogey board. Final score: Boogey board 1, Ty 0.

Constance limbers up with a bit of help from a burly partner. Better stick to construction, Mack.

Michael and Cody looking fabulous on a 10-minute R&R break.

WELCOME TO YOUR NEW HOME!

"All of a sudden, we hear people. A lot of people," says Brian Wofford. Thousands of friends and neighbors lined the streets, cheering and welcoming this deserving family.

"Hey bus driver. Move that bus!" shouts Ty.

The entire family is in shock upon viewing the new house. "When we saw that house, it hit us. Wave after wave after wave of emotion," Brian remembers. From the cascading waterfall in the front yard to the enormous house towering above it, their new home had them staring in disbelief.

Walking through the open-style downstairs is like a journey of discovery for the family. In every room they enter, there is something amazing to see. Paul's basketball-court table is a highlight. The kids are blown away by their new themed bedrooms and separate bathrooms. But no one is prepared for the unveiling of the huge upstairs gymnasium. For a family that enjoys sports, it's a dream come true.

In honor of Teresa, the Team has preserved some special memories. Out of the corner of his eye, Brian spies Teresa's desk, family photos, and her favorite pair of sunglasses.

"Honey, you are here," says Brian tearfully. When he tours his spacious new office, he lingers over the two bibles—his and Teresa's—open on the desk. "The way we lived our life."

This extreme makeover went way beyond a house.

"This is a new beginning," says Brian Wofford gratefully. "This is a new life."

It has been a hectic week, but the transformation is complete! The former matchbox-small house has been nearly doubled in space and with its coastal theme, perfectly matches its surroundings.

Home from St. Thomas, the magic continues as Brian and his family react for the first time to their new home. "I was thinking of Teresa when I saw it," says Brian. "I envisioned her happiness."

The new home is more than open enough for the entire family, and makes for wonderful opportunities for all of them to come together for meals and entertaining.

"The family needed a boost," says Brian. "Especially me. The new house brought a sense of pride and vitality."

He explains what the experience has meant. "In the past I was the 'I can do anything guy.' When Teresa passed away and I became so ill, I became the 'hang on' guy. My attitude needed adjusting. I was defeated and broken. I'm restored now. Now I'm back. The makeover stimulated the 'I can' attitude. My family has always meant everything to me. We are so grateful. The new home is perfect."

Pope FAMILY

"When Ty's bullhorn sounded at 5 A.M., that moment became etched in my heart and soul forever, like falling in love." —Caroline

Twelve-year-old Shelby Pope has a rare and debilitating condition called PMLE, or Polymorphous Light Eruption. Simply put, she is allergic to the sun.

A very active, energetic young girl until she was diagnosed with the disorder at age 5, Shelby became quite literally a prisoner in her own home. Unable to go out in the daytime without having her entire body shrouded against sunlight, Shelby can't enjoy even the simplest routine pleasures of adolescence. Exposed to sunlight, her skin breaks out in a painful rash that lasts months. Prolonged exposure will send her into shock. The family has already made two frightening visits to hospital emergency rooms.

The shock to the family was intense. A family that loved the outdoors, the Popes enjoyed camping, going to the beach, hiking, and swimming.

Since Shelby was diagnosed, however, they were forced to "sun-proof" their home. Up went heavy curtains over every window. Outdoor activities ceased. Even dinner became a dreary repetition of musical chairs as the table was moved repeatedly to avoid exposing Shelby to the rays from the setting sun.

The cost of sun-proofing the home has been enormous. But even all that was not enough. Shelby spends a huge amount of her time alone in darkness, quarantined in her tiny bedroom with sheets and blankets covering the windows. Shelby's parents, Caroline and Matthew, and her 10-year-old sister, Madison, have a wish for Shelby: That she could once again be able to enjoy the pleasures of the outdoors and be a kid again.

The Team is on its way. That wish is about to be granted.

THE TOUR

It's an amazing—and amazingly early—morning when the Team wanders up the yard holding lanterns.

"Good morning, Pope family!" bellows Ty into his bullhorn.

The Pope family bursts through the door.

After a round of hugs and expressions of joyous shock and disbelief, it's time to get to work. The Team goes on a tour.

The Pope home is a 99-year-old farmhouse with big wide windows—way too much light for Shelby. The utilities are old and worn, and there is just one bathroom. Shelby and her sister each have a small room. Shelby's windows are cloaked with large heavy blankets. The walls in Madison's room, meanwhile, are papered over with her artwork.

A former chicken farm on a large two-acre property, the Pope spread has a huge but badly rundown barn. Inside the barn is a small wine cellar the Team notices is missing a key ingredient: wine.

Ty sends the Popes on a week-long vacation to Washington, DC, where there are plenty of indoor museums for Shelby. Then the Design Team sets to work. Its goal? Make the entire property "Shelby-proof."

THE DESIGN

The Team has seven days, two-and-a-half acres, and a lot of big ideas.

The group decides almost immediately to demolish the old farmhouse and start fresh; the latest technology will be used to help give Shelby and her family their lives back.

WHERE'S THAT LIST?

"That baby is coming down! One house. One week. We'll stay up day and night. We won't eat. We won't sleep. We'll get this mission done." —Ty

That's NUTS...
AND BOLTS

"This is going to be a utility nightmare."
–Paul

WORRIED? WHO... ME?

Because Shelby's been trapped inside for so long, the Team plans for a large covered area outdoors, complete with a shaded pool, hot tub, and a real sand beach. For inside, they decide on a paint-by-numbers bedroom for Madison, the budding artist, a huge master suite for Caroline and Matthew, and a fabulous ground floor complete with a library, a parlor, dining room, and a completely new kitchen with brand new appliances.

Most importantly, they lay out a large, "safe room" for Shelby, along with a spacious sun porch that is shielded completely from the sun.

Beyond anything the Team has ever attempted, it will actually bring the outside—minus the sunlight—inside.

Ty takes on the unused barn as his secret project. His aim is to give them another usable indoor space.

The final piece of the renovation puzzle comes from Preston. While considering Shelby's predicament, he comes up with an amazing idea: harness the sun to work for, rather than against, the Popes. Solar panels installed on the roof, he suggests, will supply the family with power and reduce their utility bill to $7 per month!

MAKING IT HAPPEN

Day 2, and the Team has its design in hand when the contractor arrives to help make the dream happen. He is not alone; 60 different companies and more than 400 people will contribute to the construction of the Popes' incredible new home.

Massive equipment arrives to perform the demolition. Work goes well and the house and other utility buildings slated for removal are gone before lunch. Only the front door survives from the old house.

It will be reinstalled on the new one later.

But before any rebuilding can take place, Ty must deal with a water problem. Tests reveal high nitrate content in the water, likely due to its location on the site of a former chicken farm. The Team has no choice but to drill a

"LOTS OF THINGS ARE UNFINISHED. LET'S GO WAKE SOME PEOPLE UP. THE CLOCK IS TICKING. ONE HOUR, PEOPLE! ONE HOUR!"

—TY

new—deeper—well. As Ty discovers, the initial samples are...well...a bit less than crystal clear. Constance reassures him. And in fact, in no time fresh, clean water is flowing at a rate of 30 gallons a minute.

The workers set a grueling pace. The framers astonish the Team by working 24 hours straight. They're exhausted. Paul and Ty strap on their tool belts and pitch in to help out.

It's after four in the morning. They're hungry, too. So Paul fires up the Popes' new barbecue and cooks hamburgers and hot dogs for the entire construction crew.

Amazingly, the framing of the new two-storey farmhouse is completed.

Meanwhile, Preston is in the backyard supervising erection of an enormous sailcloth umbrella. It will cover a fantastic waterfall pool, a trampoline, a Ping-Pong table, and an outdoor cooking area. Even Preston is amazed. Shelby will have no worries walking in her backyard. And with the special U.V.-protected windows being installed in her new house, she'll be safe anywhere inside as well.

With 24 hours to go, Ty creates the perfect finishing touch. During demolition, he salvaged an aerial photograph of the property taken in 1950. He enlists a neighbor who is also a pilot to fly over the Pope property and take an updated shot from the same angle. The before and

after, framed and hung in Ty's secret barn room, show the changes the Team has made.

The final day ends in a mad scramble when the furniture arrives—three hours late.

Tracy cracks the whip and the Team falls into ranks. It's time to unload furniture people! Now get to it!

The final, most amazing piece of the puzzle is an incredible U.V.-free LED lighted ceiling that is installed in Shelby's room. Turned on, it looks exactly like a blue sky and clouds. Her room is an indoor sanctuary that feels like the great outdoors.

WELCOME TO YOUR NEW HOME!
The family is, not surprisingly, blown away.

Especially Shelby.

WE'RE NOT DONE YET!

If the success of an *EM:HE* makeover is measured in the family's reaction, then the team definitely hit the mark this time. Caroline and Matthew Pope were enchanted with their new home.

I love it.
I love it.

But the real satisfaction was not the new appliances or the extra room or the beautiful furniture. It was the new freedom they saw in their daughter's eyes. A look they have not seen in many, many years. Shelby now has a room of her own that has a window to the outdoors she had thought was gone forever. She has a safe backyard where she can socialize with friends, swim and play table tennis, and just be a kid.

"It's a dream come true."

Shelby, is a kid now. Just like any kid.

But were not done yet, folks!

It was time for Ty to reveal his secret project: the barn.

He did not disappoint. He created a spacious and sumptuous recreation room complete with an enormous— you guessed it—wine cellar.

Fully stocked, of course!

Now that is nothing to whine about!

BEFORE

"We have always had a home because our family is so close. What they did was give us a sense of accessibility, comfort, and peace that we didn't have before. Our house feels more like a home now because all our family members can enjoy every room inside and outside our home. It was so hard before, having a house that wasn't working for our family: windows Shelby couldn't sit by, a property where there was no shade or outdoor areas to shelter Shelby or for Madison to play in. Now we have it all!" —Caroline

Preston

When it comes to TV personalities, Preston Sharp is the exception, not the rule. He isn't an actor. He says what he thinks. And he eschews the spotlight.

"I'm just not into the self-promoting thing," he says. "The idea of the show is to be selfless. I feel that should permeate everything we do."

In Preston's case, it does. There may be no one on the show who invests more importance on getting things right, and less on saying the right thing.

Others on the show concur. "He's so intelligent. And he cares so much," says Paige Hemmis. "He'll look at a sconce, and if it's wrong, it upsets him. To work with someone who cares so much, it's very cool."

This attitude is not new for Preston. He has worked as a production designer on several reality shows, but he rarely if ever claims credit for it. His other design arena is the world of modernist furniture design. It is a world in which Preston has a long-established reputation for top-notch work.

"When I started doing production design in the '80s, I couldn't find the furniture I needed, so I designed it myself. And some of the paintings. I am kind of a historian of mid-century modernist furniture. I have stores in Pasadena and Hollywood. The furniture is very sought-after. I've been exhibited everywhere from museums to modernist shows."

In fact, Preston has designed everything from homes to tableware, and his furniture can be found in the homes of some of Hollywood's biggest stars.

Knowing just a little bit about Preston's background—and that's all he's really willing to share—helps to make sense of his unique character.

A fly-fishing and general sports enthusiast, he was born in Arcadia, California. His father was a scientist and intellectual. "He was everything from an orator at Northwestern, to a geologist, and an economist."

"Part of what we do has really made me look at my perception of beauty and the misconceptions of beauty," says Preston. "It broadens my concept of what true beauty is and includes people who don't use visual senses to experience beauty." He cites the case of Lance Vardon, blind and autistic, who reacted with exuberance to his new swing. That, says Preston, was a very special moment on the show.

And he was not all that pleased that Preston veered away from a career in the pure sciences. But there was also a deep appreciation for the arts in the Sharp family.

And then there was Sam Maloof. Maloof, one of America's most distinguished craftsmen, is widely revered for the beauty and design integrity of his furniture. He happened to be friends of the parents of Preston's best childhood friend. He and his friend spent hours playing on Maloof's furniture.

One of Preston's main roles on *Extreme Makeover: Home Edition* is articulating right and wrong, and pushing hard for things to be done the right way.

"I want to leave with my integrity. I'm never going to say something that is untrue."

Of all the designers on the show, Preston feels closest to Paul.

"Paulie and I have a bond that started with staying up all night to get projects finished on time. We're the ones staying up all night."

The two spend the little spare time they have on site playing music together.

And what does this man of large ideas feel at that emotional moment when the makeover is revealed to the family? Well, he's a perfectionist to the end.

"Part of me is exhausted. Part of me is anxiously awaiting the reactions of our family. And a part of me is analyzing mistakes that we should go fix."

Summing up his career, Preston puts himself in the context of his family. "The family had a couple of geniuses and two duds," he says. "I'm a dud who made a little bang."

"The guy who coined the term 'arts and sciences' is my enemy," Preston says. "There is a huge amount of science in art. Why is it easy for someone to see right and wrong in engineering, aircraft design, and automobile design? And then all of the sudden, when you reach interior design, people give up on it as scientific, and it becomes subjective. For me, it's just people's inability to articulate what is right and wrong in design."

Sharp

BEHIND THE SCENES:
The Shoot

A complete home renovation in seven days? Sounds chaotic! To the home viewer watching on television, it is. But according to Rob Day, executive in charge of production, the on-screen frenzy is nothing compared to the crazy buzz behind the scenes.

What's it like? What goes on?

First, as early as two weeks in advance of filming, crews from the location department will arrive in the neighborhood to begin asking neighbors for permission to use their property. Or "abuse," as Day wryly notes.

"It's not uncommon for us to have to repair or replace three quarters of the lawns in the immediate vicinity because of the amount of foot traffic from construction and production crews and the huge numbers of equipment either parked on them or driven over them."

The production company needs to meet local city and county officials to secure what can often be a mind-numbing blizzard of permits and clearances before film trucks and crews can arrive. Plus, accommodations must be arranged for crews that can often number as many as 400 on construction day.

It's hot work, and the crew typically plows through 50 cases of water a day. Feeding that many hungry workers is a marathon in itself. But Day says, on almost every set, neighbors are more than happy to pitch in.

"Neighbors and fans bring cakes, cookies, chili, and pretty much anything you can imagine to the cast and crew as a sign of their affection and support of the show," Day remarks.

He says the show gives away as many as 3,000 of the familiar *Extreme Makeover: Home Edition* blue t-shirts per show to the all the crews and the

Production executive Rob Day admits that a lot has changed since the first show. "Each show now is so elaborate and ambitious that hundreds of construction crew and huge pieces of equipment are needed for each renovation. Most neighborhoods we visit, we have no choice but to park our equipment on front lawns. It's a mess. We always replace what we ruin. And the community has always been very supportive. Nobody ever complains. Even at 3 A.M.!"

incredible volunteers who never fail to show up to help in any way they can.

Safety cannot be put on hold just because of a seven-day schedule, either. "We require," explains Day, "round-the-clock building inspectors from the city and county to do inspections as the work is happening so we can accomplish the build in a bit more than five days. Anyone who has done any remodeling or renovation knows this is just completely unprecedented."

For a one-hour show, Day says they typically shoot as much as 250 hours of tape!

"We utilize 21 edit bays and 19 editors to get the shows edited. We often have to turn the raw footage into a show in three or four weeks. That's why we need so many editors and bays, he explains."

As 'Reveal Day' approaches, it's not surprising that the rushed-from-the-start schedule is pushed into hyperdrive. The production and design team often go the final 36 hours

until reveal on very little—more often, no—sleep. Sometimes they might catch a nap in a truck or trailer. "One thing we can't do a build without," says Day, "is Red Bull. Lots of it!"

Finally, it's Reveal Day. Time to relax, right? Not even close. Day says crowds for this climax have grown to as many as an astonishing 10,000 fans! Organizing and controlling crowds that big on city streets is a nightmare!

The scary moments come in different shapes and sizes, however. Day recalls vividly his scariest moment. "It was Season One. A builder, who knew what our budget was for weeks, plopped down a budget in front of me the night before the "door knock" that was $250,000 more than what we had. I thought we were going to have to pack up the entire crew and equipment and go home." After hours and hours of negotiations, however, the Team found a way to make it work.

"Just another day at the office," laughs Day.

NO WAY!
What could top the amazing news that you're about to get a complete home makeover? How about seven days at a resort spa in San Diego!

Grinnan
FAMILY

"THIS WAS THE
FIRST EPISODE WE
GAVE AWAY A CAR."
—EXECUTIVE PRODUCER
TOM FORMAN

Redlands, California, is a small bustling community east of Los Angeles. But it wasn't the charms of suburban life that attracted the Grinnans to the community, however. It was the community's proximity to Loma Linda University Medical Center.

AND ONE MORE MAKES...?

TY: SO, LIKE, AT DINNER,
IT'S MUSICAL CHAIRS?
IF YOU DON'T GRAB A CHAIR
YOU'RE JUST...OUT OF LUCK?"

KATHY GRINNAN:
YEAH, BASICALLY.

Bill and Cathy Grinnan and their five children were living in a lovely home in Tucson, Arizona. It was spacious, and they loved the city. Bill was a house painter, while Cathy was a stay-at-home mom. Their joy was magnified when youngest daughter Hannah was born.

Immediately, however, things changed. Hannah was born with a rare heart defect. Doctors worried she might not survive. She needed a new heart. But it would take a miracle to locate a suitable heart for an 11-day-old baby.

It was indeed a miracle when the local Tucson hospital located a donor for little Hannah. She underwent a very risky heart transplant. The operation was successful, but there were complications as Hannah's tiny body began to reject the donor heart. Doctors determined they were not equipped to deal with Hannah's condition. They recommended to Bill and Cathy that the only place in the country that could keep Hannah alive was Loma Linda University Medical Center.

Overnight, the family was forced to make a life-altering decision. They didn't hesitate. It was unanimous. They had to do everything possible to give Hannah a shot at life. Bill quit his job. He and Cathy and their other five kids said goodbye to their extended families in Tucson, pulled up stakes, and moved to Redlands, close the medical treatment Hannah needed.

It was not exactly the happiest of homecomings. The new house is so small it can fit into the garage of the old house. With only two bathrooms for so many people, it is nonstop chaos. Space is at a premium. Rooms have to do double duty. Three of the kids sleep in the garage. It was the only house they could find, explains Bill.

Hannah is at great risk from germs and bacteria. As a transplant recipient, she needs furniture and appliance surfaces that are antibacterial and low-allergen. When she gets sick, she gets very sick. Hannah's condition has been a huge financial and emotional strain on the family. The Grinnans simply cannot afford that extreme a makeover.

Luckily, help is on the way.

THE HOUSE

"Good morning, Grinnan family!"

The Grinnans roar out of their house, whooping and cheering. The Team is amazed—shocked—that so many people have been living is such a small house. The Grinnans wholeheartedly agree! And it's about to get worse. Son Bill and his fiancé Kara will marry soon, and they don't want to leave Hannah and the family.

The house is mostly carpet, even in Hannah's room, which is a veritable dirt and bacteria factory. The backyard pool is a welcome relief in hot southern California, but Hannah is very sensitive to chlorine, so she can't really use it.

Ty sends the Grinnans on a vacation to a resort and spa in San Diego. And the Team gets to work.

Design 101

"It's not too hard to go extreme here. Basically, anything will help."
—Preston

THE RENOVATION BEGINS NOW!

Priority one for the Grinnans is more space, which is not a problem. The Team talks about building up. The problem is local zoning rules will not permit a second storey to be added onto the structure. That means an extension into the backyard. Unfortunately, that means filling in the pool.

The second priority is clean air and bacteria-free surfaces for Hannah. Carpets will be ripped out to make way for tiles and hardwood floors. And the rest of the house, including counters and furniture, will have surfaces that can be cleaned easily. Also, high-tech air filters will be installed; one for the house in general, and one in Hannah's bedroom.

This place really needed more space. Lots of new space. That was not a problem. The problem facing the Team is how to create all that new extra space and create as germ- and bacteria-free an environment for Hannah as possible.

114

The family misses Tucson, so the Team decides to bring a bit of Tucson to them in the form of a hacienda-style renovation featuring a red tile roof. If newlyweds Bill and Kara plan to live with the family, they will need a space for themselves. Ty reminds the Team not to worry about Hannah's room. He'll take care of it.

It's time for some big time demolition.

Contractors Dave and Jodi Bagwell unleash their eager crew, which begins ripping out walls, while another team is busy filling in the pool so yet another crew can pour a new foundation. But there is a problem. The cement trucks are caught in Los Angeles rush-hour traffic. Ty manages to enlist a police escort to bring the trucks in time for the overnight foundation pour, and the house stays on schedule!

On Day 2, Tracy and Michael head out together to shop for hypoallergenic pillows and mattresses, as well as furniture that can easily be wiped clean. Once the house is reframed, stainless steel countertops are installed in the kitchen. Spray foam insulation is blown into all the exterior walls. It expands into a solid, sealing the house from allergens, dust, and mold. And it's made from soybeans, so it's not harmful.

Ty munches a section just to prove it's even edible. Next, the central air-conditioning system is installed. Two HEPA exhaust filters—one in the attic and one in Hannah's closet—will scrub ambient air clean 24 hours a day. With just one day left until the Grinnans return, Ty is impressed that such a big and complicated renovation has been so successful. The house is going up like clockwork.

There are no worries, until Paul is felled by a kidney stone! But Paul is a trooper. After a quick trip to the emergency room, he is back on site—decked out in a hospital gown—to finish the job.

WELCOME TO YOUR NEW HOME!

A parade of delighted neighbors and friends throngs the street as the limousine approaches, and the Grinnans emerge for their first look at their new—and much larger—dream home.

They can't believe it's the same house!

Bill and Kathy agree the Team has captured perfectly the rugged but spectacular beauty of the Southwest in the house's earthy sunset and desert tones.

Inside they are greeted by soaring open spaces, warm rich woods, and terra-cotta style tiles that evoke the warm and dusky tones and rich contrasts of the West.

It's time to show Hannah her new room. Ty has put all his heart into this one, and he is rewarded with a huge smile from Hannah. She loves it! The bed can be entered from two sides and has small heart-shaped cutouts in each end. Reassuring images for a courageous little girl. Best of all, Hannah has nothing to fear from dangerous germs or bacteria.

The Team has installed a new pool in the backyard, and because it cleans itself without chlorine, it poses no threat to Hannah. The landscaping features faux cactus with a misting feature that will keep everyone cool on those hot summer days. Country music star Lee Ann Womack dropped by to help them inaugurate their new backyard stage!

But this was mostly all about Hannah. And the Grinnans could not have been more grateful.

"We don't pray that we get what we want," says Cathy Grinnan. "We pray that we get what we need. Thank you."

LEE ANN WOMACK!

For little Hannah, it was dream-come-true meeting.
"It was awesome. When I saw Lee Ann Womack, I hugged her."

It's the thrill of a lifetime when Bill Grinnan sits in with country music superstar Lee Ann Womack, who has generously dropped by to help welcome the Grinnans home. "It was so wonderful of her to come out here from Nashville to sing us a song," says Bill.

Coming soon...

to a **neighborhood** near **YOU!**

Vardon
FAMILY

Judy and Larry Vardon have known each other almost all their lives. And despite both of them having been severely hearing impaired since birth, they have managed to live relatively normal lives. Larry is a welder on a car assembly line. Judy is a volunteer and works with the deaf and with blind children. They have two boys, Stefan, 14, and his younger brother Lance, 12. Lance was born blind and was later diagnosed as autistic.

"What a family," recalls Executive Producer Tom Forman of the Vardons. "I can honestly say, this was one of the best weeks of my professional life. What an extraordinary family. During the reveal, I was crying like a baby."

The Vardons may be the only deaf parents in the country raising a blind and autistic child, and it presents daunting challenges. They worry constantly about emergencies and not being able to hear alarms. Lance is a very intelligent and curious child. Despite every precaution, Lance often sneaks out of the house. The police have twice found him wandering the streets. Retrofitting the entire house to make it safer is an expensive renovation, and there simply isn't the money.

In every way, Stefan is a typical teenager. He loves cars and hanging out. However, Stefan has assumed responsibilities for the family that most adults

couldn't handle. He is literally the eyes and ears for the whole family. Like any teen, he dreams of going away to college, but worries about what his absence will mean for the family.

Typically, his priorities have nothing to do with his needs, only theirs. What Stefan and the Vardons don't realize, is that hope is on the way.

THE HOUSE

When the Team's bus rolls up to the Vardon home in suburban Oak Park, Michigan, Ty surprises everyone with a unique way of greeting the family: a huge electronic sign that flashes out news of the Team's arrival.

The Team is overwhelmed with emotion when the Vardons exit the house and they meet for the first time. With Stefan acting as interpreter, the group tours the house. At less than 1,000 square feet, it's a bit cramped. The rooms are small and haphazardly arranged, which makes it difficult keeping track of Lance. Plus, how can Judy and Larry sign to one another if they cannot see across a room? The Team realizes the common space needs to be opened up.

> "This makeover is different. It's not about making it bigger or better or more fabulous. It's about making things easier for the family."
>
> —Michael

SORRY I ASKED

CONTRACTOR ADAM: WE'RE DOING OKAY.

TY: OKAY? CAN YOU BE MORE SPECIFIC?

ADAM: YOU WANT SOME DETAIL?

I'LL BUST OUT SOME DETAIL.

HEY, YO! WHO YOU GONNA CALL, DOWN THE HALL.

The three bedrooms are tiny.

The basement has been improvised into a "safe" play area for Lance. Judy has her own small room adjacent to the playroom where she does her artwork. But she must share her area with the laundry room and John's tool room. Judy is developing arthritis and would love to be able to do the laundry without having to climb up and down the stairs, always having to lock the door behind her.

This time the family vacation has some extra special significance. On their honeymoon to the Grand Hotel on Mackinaw Island, Judy and Larry could afford only lunch at the famed hotel. The Team is delighted to announce that this time around, Vardons, it's on us! Enjoy!

THE RENOVATION BEGINS NOW!

The Team realizes the priority is creating an open living space that is completely targeted to meeting the special requirements of nonhearing parents. Add to that the special needs of an autistic son and they have their work cut out for them, but no one has felt as motivated to go the extra mile as this time.

The builders, Adam Becker and Adam Helfman of Fairway Construction, arrive and signal that it's time to start demolition.

By Day 2, the frame of the new house is assembled. The Team consults special needs experts to better understand Lance's world and what they can do to help. Tracy walks blindfolded with Lance's teacher and consults with her on the design for his bedroom. Preston hears a suggestion that they create a "sensory wall" in Lance's room that features a variety of textured objects inlaid into the wall to stimulate Lance's tactile imagination.

The most important element of the renovation was to address the needs of hearing-impaired parents and a blind and autistic son. With her arthritis, for instance, it was increasingly difficult for Judy to labor up the stairs. Also, she had no way of tracking Lance's whereabouts.

TY PENNINGTON, IS HIS NAME. EXTREME MAKEOVER, IS HIS GAME. HUH!
TY: WHAT WAS THAT? WHAT JUST HAPPENED?

Forty-eight hours later, amazingly, the house is almost done. To make sure Lance is comfortable, Connie constructs an exact 3-D model of the room. She labels all of the features in Braille, and delivers the model to Lance. Allowing Lance to "feel" his room ahead of time will make it a more familiar environment.

Outside, the Team has created a new and more spacious tool room for Larry. Paul constructs an "outback bed" for Stefan. The headboard will be backlit to give the impression of a sunset over Ayers Rock, Australia!

Even hard-to-impress Preston is impressed. "Paul is probably the best designer of kids' beds and rooms I've met." Paul also builds a huge swing for Lance.

The entire interior has been fitted with an alarm system that would impress NASA, including a flashing strobe system to help Larry and Judy monitor Lance's whereabouts.

By the end of Day 5, the house is finished. Fairway Construction has set a record. Before the Vardons return, Academy Award™ winning actress Marlee Matlin arrives to help them learn a few greetings in sign language.

"He's going to love it," she says of Lance's new playroom. "You've opened a world up for him. And you'll be able to see how much he'll change, how much he'll be able to grow as a result of this!"

She is impressed with how much Stefan has sacrificed for his family. She promises Ty she will be back with a surprise.

WELCOME TO YOUR NEW HOME!

More than 6,000 friends and neighbors line the road leading up to the Vardon home. Normally, Ty encourages the crowds to cheer loudly to welcome the family home. Because the noise could frighten and confuse Lance, this time Ty teaches them to applaud in sign language, by simply raising their arms in the air and waving their hands. And as the limousine rolls up in front of the home, thousands of hands are upraised and waving.

"Welcome home, Vardon family!"

The Vardons react with sheer disbelief when they see their new house. It is beyond their expectations.

The family walks through the door, into a beautiful new home...into a new life. "It's perfect," says Judy. "It's what I've always wanted."

The family breaks down in tears when they see Lance's new playroom. Autism specialists have enthusiastically approved everything. The room includes a series of incredible toys for Lance that will help his developmental skills and provide a lot of fun. And there is a small wall cubbyhole with soft textures and black lights where he can escape when he needs alone time.

Judy speaks for Lance. "Thank you!"

Stefan is stunned by his new car-themed bedroom. "Awesome! I love it."

As much as this makeover was about Lance and his special needs, it was also about recognizing the extraordinary sacrifices Stefan has made over the years for his family. A new home was only the beginning. Marlee Matlin returns with good friend, Bill Austin, chairman of the Starkey Hearing Foundation.

Bill presents Stefan with a $50,000 university scholarship.

"I cried," Stefan says. "It just really affected my future from that day forward. It's just the best experience of my life."

WE'RE NOT DONE YET!

A huge part of therapy for an autistic child is to keep the senses stimulated. The Team took those needs into account when they came up with a sensory-rich bedroom and playroom for Lance. The walls feature touchable extrusions and there is a cubby hole for Lance to escape into when he needs to feel safe.

Older brother Stefan has sacrificed just about everything to help his family and has asked for nothing in return. He was even willing to abandon hopes of going to college. But because of a generous donation, Stefan has no worries about college—or that his family will be okay.

Paige *Hemmis*

There may be no woman in the history of television with Paige Hemmis' combination of beauty and skills. A statuesque blond with a killer smile, she could turn heads with her looks alone. But it's when she fires up a reciprocating saw and starts to rip sheets of plywood that people really stop and stare. Outfitted with her trademark pink tool belt, Paige is a traditional girl with a fearless attitude. And she's a fine carpenter to boot.

Born in Wisconsin and raised in Chatsworth, California, Paige was "a real tomboy" as a child, always taking risks and trying new things. And that really hasn't changed much. "My parents taught me that I could be whatever I wanted to be." In many ways, they led by example. Her father is an entrepreneur and a former racecar driver. "He started different businesses every few years." Her mother is an investor. "My father is very risky and my mom is very conservative," she says. Paige considers herself a mix of the two.

And it shows in the life she has chosen. When she isn't working as a carpenter on *Extreme Makeover: Home Edition*, she's training to be a stunt driver for films and commercials. A psychology and theology grad from University of California, Santa Barbara, she has been a teacher, a medical technician, a world-traveling sales representative, a real-estate entrepreneur, and a wedding planner. "I feel like everything that I have done has prepared me for what I do now," she says.

It was her work as a wedding planner that indirectly led to her role on *Extreme Makeover: Home Edition*. Helping families with the biggest day of their lives led naturally into the idea of helping people obtain their first homes. So Paige and her husband co-founded Rent to Own Investments. Rent to Own buys houses, renovates them, and develops innovative rent-to-own solutions for tenants who cannot afford the steep down payment required to purchase.

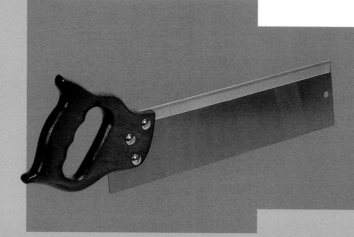

It's fitting that, for Paige, being a cast member of a show that changes people's lives has changed hers as well.

"It's definitely made me busier. I'm not home as much. But it's also enhanced and enriched my life more than I ever thought a job could. It's taken my charity work and made it a job."

When she and her husband got into the business, they knew little of construction or carpentry. That soon changed. "We had enough money to buy the houses, but not enough to pay someone to fix them up."

It's a common quandary. And Paige tackled it head on. "We bought a fix-it 1-2-3 book, and we learned. I was doing framing, drywall, and roofing. That's where you learn the skills you need to take creativity and make it reality. You can take as many courses as you want, but until you actually get out there and do it and make mistakes, you don't really learn." She also became a fan of home remodeling shows and began to pursue opportunities to participate as a guest carpenter. She appeared on *Monster House*, where she was discovered by the producers of *Extreme Makeover: Home Edition*.

Her work with Rent To Own has also taught her something about human nature, and how much people appreciate help when they're down.

For a carpenter on *Extreme Makeover: Home Edition*, the workload is enormous. In a given week, Paige can be required to construct more than half a dozen projects for the home. "It's very rewarding because you know the family is going to enjoy what you've made."

Her favorite project? "The pirate ship room and pirate ship bed I built for the McCrory family. It was a complete pirate ship that looked like it faded into the wall. I worked with Luan, a bendable kind of wood. And I got to work with a muralist. That was so much fun."

Ed

A native of London, Ed Sanders was enjoying a successful career as an actor and television host in England just two short years ago. He appeared on the successful soccer drama *Dream Team* and was in his third season as host of *Fear Factor UK*. The problem was, his American wife Gioia missed home, so Ed and his family packed up and moved to the U.S.

"We were going to move to Miami, start a business, and commute to the U.K. for acting jobs," says Ed. "But my wife said if you're going to go to America, why don't we just go to California—you can try and pursue acting there. So we moved to California and got an agent and I looked for acting work. I wasn't successful for the first couple of months, but then an audition came up for *EM:HE*."

The rest, as they say, is history.

Ed and Gioia, together with their 3-year-old son Max, have decided to make California their permanent home. When necessary, Ed commutes to acting jobs in the U.K. The family has fallen in love with Southern California, and with its sandy beaches in particular.

"To build a house in a year takes a lot of teamwork," Ed Sanders explains, "but to build a house in the five days and nine hours we have every week, everyone has to be pulling in the same direction. To be honest, I still don't know how we do it!"

But he's glad they do.

"I grew up in London, and we were about 50 miles from the nearest beach, but my parents used to take us to the beach all the time, every weekend," Ed says. "Living in California with my wife and my son, we go down to the beach at the Balboa Peninsula near Newport every weekend. We just chill out there, you know, go in the sea, build sandcastles, have a picnic lunch. You can just go there with your family and relax," he says, "even when it's cloudy and overcast. But hey, that's considered a sunny day in London!"

With the long days they work, the usually sleep-deprived cast and crew try to keep things light during tapings, so Ed and his fellow cast and crew members like to have a little fun at one another's expense. "When you're trying to do a link to camera and you've got a crew member doing stupid stuff behind the camera to crack you up, things can get a little crazy. Being able to joke that's what keeps you going."

Ed is thrilled that his first acting job in America has turned out to be on a hit show. He credits *EM:HE*'s success to the incredible chemistry between the team members and their dedication to the values of the show.

"Teamwork is the key word for this show," he says. "We would never get this done in a million years without teamwork. And I'm not just talking about the designers, construction workers, the plumbers, and the electricians. I'm talking about the caterers, the guys who clean the toilets and remove the litter, the local police department that sometimes rushes materials to the site when we're behind, the neighbors that help out, the family members that come down and help paint, stain, varnish, polish, dust, vacuum—just one massive team. It's incredible really."

The feeling of helping others, Ed says, more than makes up for the draining schedule and stress that sometimes comes with it. And when his career ends some day, he says, *EM:HE* is a show he will look back on with pride, knowing he was part of something that changed whole families' lives.

"This is like no other show I've ever done—and I've done a lot of shows in my time," he says. "I've done shows where I've given away money, but I've never done a show before that has changed somebody's life. You give away a few thousand pounds, and it's great, but this is changing someone's entire life. I still can't imagine what it must feel like to wake up the following day in a brand new 5,000-square-foot house, completely decked out, with everything imaginable, every appliance known to man. I always say I feel like a little angel without wings," he laughs. "It's tiring work, but it's worth it.

"The good thing is, at the end of the day, and I know it sounds corny, we really help a lot of families, which is what this show is all about. It's a great thing."

Ed and his wife and young son have left England behind and taken to the beaches of California. The beach is the perfect place to unwind and recharge after the rigors of an *EM:HE* production, even if fans of the show often recognize Ed. "The fans are very respectful. They just come up and ask if they can talk or take a photo. It's wonderful."

Sanders

It's been a tough haul for Jennifer Elcano, running a farm on her own and raising two kids. She wondered how to make ends meet. Or even if she could make ends meet. Help is on the way.

Elcano FAMILY

The Elcano family of Bakersfield, California, has operated the same 20-acre family farm for the last 100 years. Up until recently, Glen and Jennifer Elcano were running the farm with their two children, 11-year-old Michael and 6-year-old Ashley. It was tough going; sometimes it was hard to make ends meet. Their love for the farm, however, was as deep as their love for each other. Glen and Jennifer stuck together and made it work.

The 100-year-old farmhouse had been a dream for Jennifer and Glen. But after Glen died tragically and unexpectedly, the dream turned into a nightmare. Any hopes of restoring the old house vanished and now the house is a painful reminder to Jennifer of Glen and his dream of a working farm.

Until a few months ago.

Glen was on his way home from making a delivery at a neighboring farm when a car pulled out in front of him. He was killed instantly in the collision.

"I lost my best friend that day," remembers Jennifer of her high-school sweetheart.

Running a family farm is difficult at the best of times. The work is backbreaking and the hours long. Family farmers aren't rich, either. Suddenly, Jennifer was a grieving widow who had inexplicably lost the love of her life. It was unbearable. But neither she nor her kids could quit. There were still hundreds of chores to be done. With Glen gone, in fact, they would have to work even harder.

Every nickel they could scrape together—every ounce of energy—Jennifer has been plowing back into keeping the farm afloat. The beautiful 100-year-old farmhouse that Glen and Jennifer had dreamed of restoring is in danger of falling in on top of them. As is their dream of operating a family farm.

Like Glen, soon it, too, might be just a memory. Jennifer and her kids need help.

"This was a really different episode for us because their loss was so fresh," recalls Executive Producer Tom Forman.

"We were used to a world where people are excited and ready to jump up and down and hug Ty. And that is just not where this family was at, at all. It had only been four short months since the death of her husband. Four months since these kids had lost their father. But we watched a community rally to help one it its own. They were incredible. Absolutely amazing."

THE HOUSE

Ty shouts, "Good morning, Elcano family!" and Jennifer—her hand clamped over her mouth in speechless gratitude—greets the Team and introduces Michael and Ashley.

Delighted that her prayers were answered, Jennifer and her kids are mindful of the circumstances. Glen was a very special man: a loving husband and devoted father. As Jennifer tours the house with the Team, it is obvious how much he is missed. And what a rough road it has been trying to keep the farm solvent in his absence.

The house appears no less stressed than Jennifer.

Constructed with no foundation, the weathered and badly fatigued farmhouse looks like it could keel over in the next gust of wind. There simply has been no time to deal with the clutter. Windows won't open. Floors are warped and need refinishing. Doors refuse to swing clean on their hinges. Walls slump exhausted. The house is cramped and tumbledown. Invasive weeds have insinuated themselves through dozens of cracks and are literally growing up inside the walls.

Surveying the surroundings, it is clear to the Team that this will be more than a brick-and-mortar renovation.

With no time or money to plant, Jennifer hastily improvised a business buying and reselling hay. It's a lot of work and the profit margin is razor-thin. The only long-term solution is planting all 20 acres. But that will take a lot of time and effort. And money. None of which Jennifer has.

"My family has always been very important to me. I just wasn't sure how I was going to go on without my husband in my life and my kids without their dad."

The Team needed to address the same sadness and fatigue in the house. It, too, looked like it had lost all hope.

The house looked its age. The windows did not open. The walls warped and sagged. Wind whistled through the cracks and weeds were growing inside the walls. It needed a new roof.

It, and Jennifer, needed a lift.

The Team realizes it's time to plant some seeds of its own—Extreme Makeover seeds! And there is not a minute to lose. While Ty wishes Jennifer and her kids well on their vacation trip to Disneyland, the Team gets to work.

THE RENOVATION BEGINS NOW!

It's unanimous: the Elcano house must come down. The only question is what will go up in its place. The Team ambitiously explores the possibility of a brand new and spectacularly spacious 2,000-square-foot red barn house.

The new design calls for an open kitchen and dining area. All new appliances, of course, as well as a luxurious living room. Michael is crazy about reptiles. He has a few in his room already.

Paul and Preston "hatch" a plan that will turn Michael's room into a reptile-lover's dream bedroom. But it will be important that Michael have some special memory of his father. Something he can cherish and call his own. The two designers think they have the perfect solution.

Meanwhile, Tracy and Constance find inspiration for Ashley's new bedroom in her love for all things cowgirl.

Last but not least, the Team decides Jennifer needs a new bedroom that will allow her a private sanctuary from all the stress and pressure and worry of running the farm on her

IT'S 11:59: DO YOU KNOW WHERE YOUR NEW HOME IS?

"You need to kick it into gear, sweet-stuff!"

The Team arrives early that morning to deliver the good news. As with so many makeover projects, the crew digs in to do whatever needs to be done. Hundreds of friends of the Elcanos turned out to generously help replant the fields and load the new barn with enough hay to get Jennifer and the farm on their feet.

Ty figures the new barn will be much too big to hide behind the Team bus for the unveiling, so he decides to call in some superstar help.

"I had to make a phone call. Actually, I called Randy Travis 'Randy? Hey, man. It's Ty. Listen, I kind of need help. A favor. So...you've got a bus, right?'"

"Yeah..."

RANDY TRAVIS!

Country music legend and superstar Randy Travis proves that he knows his way around more than just a guitar. Dropping by the site to lend a hand, the Team discovers he has some smooth moves with a hammer. He generously volunteers to stage a benefit concert for the good folks of Bakersfield, and they raise $60,000 for a fund for Jennifer and her kids.

own. Not to mention the extra stress of single-parenting. Grieving is a long process. Jennifer needs a place to be serene, to remember, and be at peace.

Ty tells the Team not to worry about Jennifer's office makeover. That will be his secret project.

Day 2 begins with the arrival of contractor Todd Sweaney and his gung-ho crew of 150 sledgehammer-wielding demolition professionals.

Ty, however, surprises them with a surprise demolition "expert" of his own! An enormous tractor with which he hopes to literally pull the house down.

"A little tractor pull, if you know what I'm saying."

Cool idea! The only problem? It doesn't work. The tractor isn't powerful enough. So Ty brings in some really heavy-duty machinery to do the pulling, and in a matter of seconds, what was once the Elcano house is nothing but rubble.

Sweaney and his team begin construction of the barn and the house simultaneously. Tracy heads off to shop for furniture and décor. Ty, meanwhile, goes on a recruiting mission. He visits Scott, a neighbor and fellow farmer, and one of Glen's best friends. They discuss plans for replanting the fields with alfalfa.

What this project is all about is partnership and cooperation. Farmers helping farmers. Neighbors helping neighbors. Craftsmen and workers—even some celebrities—moved by a family's tragedy to do whatever they can to help out. It's not about egos, it's about coming to the aid of family.

Scott happily obliges and makes a few calls. Suddenly, practically the entire town of Bakersfield turns up at the Elcano farm. The all-volunteer Elcano Army heads out on a flotilla of tractors to till the soil and plant 20 acres of alfalfa.

The renovation is in high gear, and Ty is cautiously optimistic that the Team and crew will finish in time. But it would be great to have a little extra help.

Like maybe some superstar help?

When county music sensation Randy Travis shows up unexpectedly, the Team and crew nearly drop their hammers in shock. Travis has heard about the Elcanos and their problems, and he wants to help.

Not only is Travis handy with a guitar, he proves very quickly that he knows his way around a hammer and nails, too! Travis, however, has his own idea how he might add his own special touch to the renovation: a concert for the crew and local residents to help raise money for the Elcanos.

From the thousands of wildly appreciative fans who turn out to hear Travis perform his latest hits, it's a sure bet the idea was a good one. When he plays his new single, "Four Walls," the crowd is deeply moved. It seems to speak to the very life that Glen and Jennifer Elcano were living on the farm.

"Four walls, three words, two hearts, and one love," he sings. The concert raises an astonishing $60,000 dollars.

By Day 6, the house is almost finished. The brand new barn is a huge improvement. Except for one minor detail—it's empty.

What good is a hay barn with no hay?

The Team puts the word out that they need some hay—and FAST! Soon farmers from all over the state are trucking in with load after load of hay to fill the barn. Only a few hours left before the family comes home. What a difference seven days can make when friends come to the aid of a neighbor.

Ty sums it up: "GlenJen Farms is back in business, people!"

OH MY...

WELCOME TO YOUR **NEW HOME!**

Hundreds of cheering friends have turned out to line the dusty dirt road that leads to the Elcano farm. When Jennifer climbs out of the limousine and Ty shouts, "Move that bus!" she is so amazed at the transformation she drops halfway to her knees.

"This is like a dream," she whispers.

Inside, she is overwhelmed with emotion. The Team has salvaged a pair of Glen's boots and placed them beside the new fireplace. Michael sees them first.

"Look at the fireplace, Mom! Dad's boots."

For Jennifer, the boots mean everything. "It feels like he is here with us."

Ashley's new bedroom, appropriately, has been outfitted in cowgirl-chic—complete with a real leather saddle.

For Michael, the Team took his love of reptiles to the extreme. They install two walls that are giant terrariums. There is another terrarium at the head of his bed. But there is

"It is hard for me to put my feelings into words. I never imagined that this could actually happen to us. It is such a wonderful feeling to come home every day and see this house and know that someone cared enough about you to make it happen."

—Jennifer Elcano

more. Before Glen died, he and Michael had been working on a model wooden airplane. They never had a chance to finish. Hanging from his ceiling is the same model airplane—finished —just as he and his dad would have wanted.

Out back Ty unveils the new barn, filled with 15,000 bales of fresh hay. Plus a little something to help haul all that hay around: a new Ford F-250 Super Duty truck.

Jennifer's new office has been relocated to the front of the house where she can see the trucks load and unload the hay. Most importantly, a cherished framed photo of Glen hangs on the wall as a constant reminder to Jennifer that he will be with her always.

"I wish that my husband could be here to see all of this. All of his dreams have come true. I feel very blessed."

"I definitely feel more optimistic about life. I know that we can continue with the business that my husband worked so hard to build and that our children will be taken care of. I knew the day we came home that everything was going to be okay. We know that he is here with us, even though we can't see him."

"My kids miss their dad very much. It feels so good to put smiles on their faces."
—Jennifer Elcano

Michael Moloney

"I don't think anybody knew what we had or what we were going to do until we put this concept for a show together with this group of people. And this thing happened. It's like a gift, to be a part of this."

Michael Moloney was born to design. From his work to his personal life and everything in between, there is a love of design behind just about everything he does. Even when Michael was growing up in Palos Verdes Estates, California, where he loved designing his bedroom as a youngster, getting things to look just right was always important to him.

"At my Mom's house I was always worried about what went with what and where. It seems like I was always into designing," he says.

At the age of 16, Michael entered the fashion business, working as a model, photographer, and designer. During a stint as a manufacturer's sales rep, he bought a shop in Redondo Beach, California, that specialized in refurbished second-hand home furnishings and antiques. Rechristened Le Garage, the shop was a huge success, and it enabled him to open a high-end furnishings store called Maison Luxe a block from the ocean in Manhattan Beach.

It was at Maison Luxe that Michael first made the contacts that led to a series of television appearances. "I had a couple of clients who always said, 'You need to be on television, you have the personality for it.'" The clients set Michael up with an audition for a new home makeover show called *Clean House.* The show's producers thought he was a natural fit.

The *Clean House* feature made Michael a natural choice when it came time to cast *Extreme Makeover: Home Edition.* "It was just one of those things that was so obvious in a way," he says. "It just seemed like the right combination for everyone."

Michael credits his fellow cast members and everyone behind the scenes for *EM:HE*'s incredible success. "It's an amazing group of people. Nobody is showing up to just do a job, everybody really cares. They care about the families,

Michael points to the Vardon family episode from Season Two as one of his favorites. "Their little house was probably the simplest redo we've ever done. It's still a very modest home. But the story, how it was handled and the way it shows what people go through, for me, it made clear what we're doing," he says. "It was just an amazing story, an amazing family."

In his free time, Michael loves to travel, combining it with design, as usual. "To me it's all about aesthetics. Like when I go to Paris, everything there is beautiful. It's the architecture; it's the experiences of being with the people in a restaurant," he says. "All of that relates back to design, too, for me. I just love to travel and see the world and have as many experiences as I can. It's my biggest hobby and my greatest passion outside of design work."

they care about design, they care about what's right and what's going to be best," he says. "I think that these are things that make our show such a beautiful thing. For some reason we got blessed with this cast of characters, and believe me, they're all characters, who together really create something very special."

"You have to give a lot of credit to the people you don't see, the hundreds of people we travel with on a weekly basis. Our cameramen and our producers and our design producers, the sound people and the makeup people, the coordinating producers, everybody that is involved," Michael says. "Everybody is so vested. When you're doing good things it all trickles down and everybody gets affected by it. And it's showing other people what can be done with enough people who have one goal in mind. It's pretty amazing."

As far as the impact the show has on the lives of the families it helps, Michael had an epiphany of sorts a few days into the filming of the pilot Powers family episode.

"I remember walking up the street towards the house and realizing the magnitude of what we were doing. I just got completely emotional because this was something that was going to change lives. Suddenly I was just overwhelmed."

"I've had a lot of moments," Michael says. "I'm not afraid to shed a tear. I think once you open your emotional floodgates and realize it's okay to cry, it feels good and it's cathartic ."

BEHIND THE SCENES:
Family Producer

Once the cameras are shut down and the taping is over and the crew has moved on to another site for a new show, the work for Family Producer Herb Ankrom has just begun.

"When we leave the family to their new home," he explains, "it doesn't end there. I keep in touch with all the families on a regular basis, and help them to a certain extent maintain and get used to their new space."

With a crazy seven-day schedule, it's inevitable that unexpected problems might occur—a leaky window, a shower that doesn't work—and it's Ankrom's job to make sure those problems are fixed as quickly as possible.

"Our contractors are amazing and guarantee everything, so the family has very little to worry about."

It's a job that for Ankrom has become personal.

"In a small way these families have become an extension of my own family. I get e-mails and phone calls from them informing me of weddings and report cards as well as random acts of kindness done long after we are gone by the community to help the family."

His job begins when a family has been selected by ABC for a featured renovation.

"I am responsible for planning and expediting the vacation as well as any special events that happen during a taping, such as celebrity guest or fund-raising events. And when a family returns to the home, I am with them to get them settled and adjusted to their new environment."

Ankrom meets with the family the night before the "reveal," he explains. With so much going on and so many opportunities for schedules to go awry, it's insurance against disaster. On one episode, for instance, foul weather stranded a returning family for 18 hours in the airport.

"In this job, you have to learn how to be creative about solving problems," he joked.

Despite the constant chaos and the endless travel and long hours that are the reality of a television show, Ankrom cherishes most the small off-camera moments that reveal why this show is different.

Herb Ankrom

"I was in Atlanta with the Harper family," he remembers. "It was the morning of the reveal and the kids really wanted to have McDonald's muffins. I took the kids and Mr. Harper, in the dead of winter, down the street from the Ritz Carlton where we were staying for some breakfast. After I had gotten all of them food, I noticed Milton Harper at the counter ordering more food, so I jumped up and offered to pay because the family is our guest."

Ankrom said Harper politely but firmly demurred. "'No thank you,' he said. 'This one is on me. Today I am going to receive a great gift, and in a small way, this is how I can begin to repay all that has been done for me.'"

Ankrom said Milton Harper then proceeded to buy a meal for nine homeless people who had come into the restaurant to keep warm.

"It may sound a little cheesy or contrived," he says, "but it is these moments that make all the hours, stress, and absence from home worthwhile."

Family Producer Herb Ankrom's work behind the scenes ensures that everything goes smoothly before, during—and after—the shoot. He's the problem solver and he finds his work intensely personal. "These families have become an extension of my own family," he says.

"For the first time," says Lucy Ali, "I felt...there was going to be hope."

The family's experience renovating their home has been a nightmare. That is about to change.

Ali FAMILY

Lucy Ali is the mother of two bright, healthy, intelligent 12-year-old boys, Paul and Kuran. It wasn't always the case. Lucy adopted both boys as drug-addicted infants. Lucy isn't rich. But she is rich in spirit and generosity.

Last year Lucy, decided to renovate their tiny house in Queens, New York. She secured a bank loan and hired a contractor. She trusted that the contractor would help realize her special dream for her two boys: a beautiful and comfortable renovated house they could call "home."

The contractor arrived, ripped the house apart, and then disappeared. He stole their money. He stole their hope. He stole their dream. The Ali family was left with nothing—no money and no place to live. The family shuffled from one place to the next, and even spent some time at a homeless shelter until they were kicked out because, technically, Lucy was still a homeowner.

Eventually, Lucy found an attic apartment a few miles away. Crammed on top of each another like sardines, the family was caught in a frustrating limbo. Forced to pay rent on the attic apartment, Lucy had to keep up mortgage payments on the house. The bills piled up and up, and they had nowhere to turn.

fabulo-meter

BIG...BIG...BIG. It needs to like, if you cranked it up, it would **BLOW** you out of your chair. —Michael

THE HOUSE

When the Team arrives on site, they are appalled. The so-called contractor has left the house in ruins. It's a disaster. Walls have been ripped down and nails poke through like porcupine quills. Incompetent workmen have sliced through or torn off plumbing and electrical lines. Debris is piled everywhere.

The third floor is an open-air skeleton of half-framed walls. To their horror, the Team discovers that the house sags dangerously on its foundation.

The Team has a very big job ahead. But before the family is whisked away on a dream vacation, Ty makes Lucy a promise. This time around, she will not be disappointed.

THE RENOVATION BEGINS NOW!

The Team huddles up to create a plan that both meets Lucy's dream-home concept and corrects the structural damage done by the incompetent contractor. The Team realizes that in many ways this is as much building an entirely new home as it is renovating an existing home.

They settle on a plan that features simple, clean lines, and lots of greens, blues, and sages, Lucy's favorite colors. In addition to adding lots of new space and more rooms, the Team comes up with a few inspired flourishes. Ty adopts Lucy's bedroom as his secret project.

There's no time to waste.

No sooner has the crew launched into its demolition, however, than work stops abruptly.

It turns out, the former contractor has unsafely framed an entire second-storey addition on top of an old wall. The entire addition is being held up by nothing more than four slender two-by-fours. Before any work can resume, the wall needs to be reinforced.

The new frame goes up very fast. Ty is delighted to report the project is ahead of schedule.

The front porch is ripped away, and in the rubble, the Team discovers a surprisingly rich treasure trove of odd and interesting artifacts, including old bottles, books, even an old banjo! Paul and Preston decide to somehow incorporate the curios into the new design.

By Day 3, the framing is finished and the plumbers and electricians are crawling over the house like an army of ants. The Team cannot remember when a renovation has been so much ahead of schedule. Over the next 48 hours, Team and crew make excellent progress.

IS SOMEONE MISSING A DESIGNER?

"We're looking at this house that needs a ton of work. And we have no contractor. We're a bit worried." —Paul

Renovation comes to halt when it is discovered that the entire upper floor has been built on top of an unreinforced wall. The area is so dangerous that the crew is ordered out until supports can be hoisted into place.

145

WELCOME TO YOUR NEW HOME!

The Ali family is stunned at their first glimpse of their wonderful new home. "For the first time," explains Lucy, "I felt like there was going to be hope because God made a way where there was no way."

The new house features a beautiful and spacious new kitchen. Happily, Lucy lingers for a sweet moment over the granite countertop. The boys are knocked out when they come into their new ultimate media room, which includes an enormous flat-screen plasma television, massive speakers, and state-of-the-art computer games and DVD technology.

Since Paul dreams of being an actor, his new bedroom was styled after a glittering and glamorous Broadway theater. For that touch of authenticity, Paul DiMeo managed to decorate the room in fabric and carpet straight from the hit musical, *The Lion King*.

Kuran is set on being an architect, so his room features a unique protractor-shaped bed and large drafting table. Lucy loves her new bedroom. For someone who has spent so much time and energy meeting the needs of others, Lucy finally has a wonderful and sumptuous sanctuary of her own.

The most ambitious makeover, however, might be the backyard. Paige has wowed the family with the crazy idea of creating a go-kart track for the boys. The boys can't wait to hop into the driver's seat!

"They haven't been able to play in their backyard for two years," said Paige.

Before, Lucy had to sleep in a chair because there was no room for a proper bed. Neither she nor her two boys have to worry now about making do.

Their new home is open and spacious and there is plenty of room for all three of them— and a beautiful big bed for Lucy.

Mackey

FAMILY

When Consuela Mackey broke a foot playing sports back in 1980, she became acutely aware of how difficult life can be. She came to understand the problems people with disabilities must struggle with every day. She founded the non-profit organization Operation Confidence to try to change perceptions and improve resources for people with disabilities.

Twenty-five years later, Operation Confidence continues to provide job training and individualized training in personal care and education on workplace etiquette to hundreds of individuals with disabilities, helping them to find jobs, and assimilate into the workplace.

Consuela's commitment doesn't end at 5 o'clock. She has opened up her house as a sort of drop-in center for the disabled community. Many nights she has even given up her bed to a client in need, and slept on a chair.

In addition to raising grandson Eric since he was a baby and niece Valada since she was 6 years old, Consuela has been mother to many foster kids over the years. Recently, Consuela opened her home to her sister Sandra and Sandra's teenage daughter, Georgia. Sandra is going blind, and Consuela is teaching her how to handle life with reduced vision.

Consuela's only source of income is a small beauty shop. Whatever profit comes from that goes mostly to fund Operation Confidence and the mounting bills of caring for an extended family.

Her modest house, unfortunately, is not as robust as Consuela herself. When the Team arrives at the Mackey home in Granada Hills, California, it's immediately obvious that the house is showing signs of major stress and fatigue.

Consuela and her family react to news that they will be getting an extreme home makeover!

"It's time that Consuela has a place that gives her confidence." —Michael

THE HOUSE

The Mackey house has been pushed beyond its limits. There are glaring design problems that need to be addressed. For starters, the front door isn't wide enough to admit a wheelchair. Many of the disabled people who arrive have to leave their chairs outside and be carried into the home. The kitchen, which must serve all of Consuela's extended family and Operation Confidence clients, is tiny.

Window frames need replacing. The roof is a patchwork of holes and will need replacing, too. The ceiling is dangerously warped and could cave in at any moment.

Since Sandra and Georgia moved in, there are not enough bedrooms for everyone, so mother and daughter share a bed in one room. In another bedroom, Eric sleeps on a mattress cantilevered across a dresser. Consuela's room— a small office in one corner, and her bed a few feet away—is the most burdened space in the house.

Out back sits Consuela's old truck. She used it every day for 10 years to pick up food from the Children's Hunger Fund and deliver it to families that didn't have anything to eat. She doesn't give up on things that are run down, she explains, so the Team pledges not give up on her truck, either.

Ty wishes them a great trip to a resort in Playa Del Carmen, Mexico for a well-deserved week of relaxation.

It's time for the Team to get to work.

"THERE WAS AN ... UNFORTUNATE...DESIGN FLAW. HOW TO SOLVE THE "WINDOW LOOKS DIRECTLY FROM THE STREET INTO THE BATHROOM" PROBLEM. WE DID SOME FRANTIC LAST-MINUTE WINDOW TINTING, HOWEVER. WHEW."
—EXECUTIVE PRODUCER TOM FORMAN

THE RENOVATION BEGINS NOW!

More space! It's a familiar objective. This time around, however, the Team has the added element of accessibility to consider. Ty is amazed at how much Consuela has accomplished in her tiny bedroom office. So he takes her new office on as his secret project.

The Team and crew flip into overdrive. The house needs new walls and a new roof. The new walls will provide lateral strength and stability against earthquakes. The Team plan has absolutely maxed out all available space.

Ty, however, is at loggerheads trying to figure out where to put Consuela's new office. Problem solved when contractor Matt Plaskoff finds the perfect office space about 20 minutes away. A few days of intense activity later and the house is nearly finished. With less than a day until the family returns, the Team launches into its patented full-court press to get the house finished.

The Team can help a woman who is always there to help others. "Just because you're in bad shape, that doesn't mean you get thrown away," says Paul. "Consuela certainly believes that. You're in bad shape, you get some confidence and get back out there."

WELCOME TO YOUR NEW HOME!

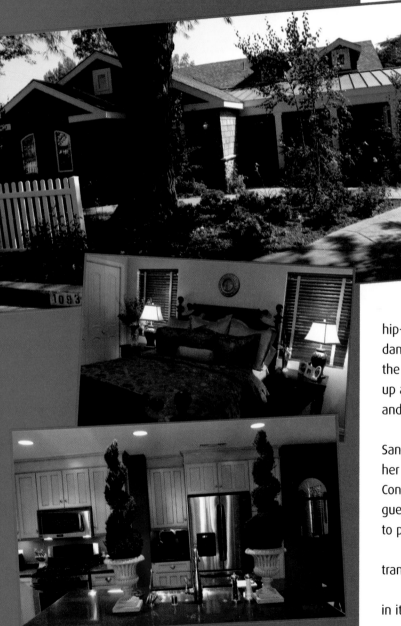

This makevoer is going to be what I like to refer to as 'over the top'." —Michael

When the limousine turns down the block and passes the hundreds of friends and neighbors gathered to welcome them back, Consuela Mackey can't believe her eyes.

"Move that bus!" shouts Ty as the bus pulls away and the family glimpses its new home for the first time. Counsela is so overcome with emotion she collapses. Grandson Eric catches her in his arms.

The Design Team opened up the interior, allowing easy wheelchair access throughout the house. Outside, level paving-stone pathways and a patio allow full access. There is a barbecue and, to one side of the house, a luxurious water garden.

Since Georgia is into hip-hop, her bedroom features a hip-hop princess theme, complete with a round bed, a lighted dance-floor, and a disco ball. Eric loves trucks. Paul gave him the ultimate guy pad, with a hydraulic bed that he can move up and down with a remote control, a wall mural of a truck, and a huge hot tub.

Valada and Sandra each have their own elegant bedroom. Sandra's features a large television that she can see even with her limited vision. Spacious and cool, and designed to pamper, Consuela's master bedroom includes a fold-down bed for guests. Wondering where her office might be, Ty is delighted to present her the keys to her new and much larger office.

Her old rundown truck out back has been magically transformed into a fully renovated and customized beauty!

A treasured photo of Consuela's father and mother sits in its place of honor just inside the front door.

"As soon as you come in, before you enter into any part of my house, you're being blessed by my parents and I love that," says Consuela.

Burns

FAMILY

Jerry and Ellen Burns have three children: Pam, 17, Jeff, 16, and their youngest son, 6-year-old Ben. As bright and energetic as any 6-year-old, Ben has one thing that most kids don't: osteogenesis imperfecta—a rare genetic disorder characterized by brittle bones. Ask Ben, and he'll tell you his bones are made of glass. He has already broken more than 20 bones in his body.

At first, social services accused Ellen and Jerry of abuse and removed Ben from the house. It was a nightmare. Jerry and Ellen had no idea why their son's bones were breaking so easily and so often. But to be accused of abusing him! It was only after a battery of tests that they heard the diagnosis. Delighted to have their infant son returned, Ellen admits, it was a sad and brutal diagnosis.

Jerry and Ellen had to come to terms with the fact that the house itself posed a constant threat to Ben. The simplest fall could shatter a leg. Because of the risk from falling, Ben crawls around on his knees. Outdoors he uses a sit-down walker. Ellen's sister Diana moved in to help out.

Over the years, Jerry and Ellen Burns have done everything they can for Ben. The family has made every sacrifice. It hasn't been enough. All they want is a safe home for Ben. They need help.

IT'S 11:59:
DO YOU KNOW WHERE YOUR NEW HOME IS?

Michael: Where is everybody?
Paul: I don't know.
Michael: The house is a work in progress. Now it comes to a screeching halt.
I'm a bit, well, let's just say I'm concerned.

THE HOUSE

"Good morning, Burns Family!"

Needless to say, the shocked Burns family greets the arrival of the Team to their house in Garden Grove, California, with shouts of joy.

Inside, the Team realizes instantly why Jerry and Ellen are so concerned. The interior is a veritable land mine of danger. Nothing but sharp angles, hard surfaces, and an absolutely unforgiving concrete floor! Renovating the house from tip to toe to make it "Ben-friendly" will be a real challenge. The juggle of six people and four bedrooms needs to be addressed, too.

While the Team puts on its thinking cap, Ty sends the grateful family off to a luxurious week-long vacation at a resort spa in San Diego.

THE RENOVATION BEGINS NOW!

Architect Karen Braitmayer is called in for a consultation. She has osteogenesis imperfecta, too. Her suggestion is a house that encourages Ben to stay active. Karen and the Team come up with a design that maximizes open spaces and low-impact cushioned surfaces, and has handrails throughout. Swimming is one of the few activities that does not put Ben's bones at risk. The Team insists on a backyard pool.

With some surprise celebrity help on demolition day, the crew makes short work and soon the framing of the renovation begins.

Cushioned flooring is laid throughout the house. Walls are coated with a special additive to soften impact and on Ben's walls the Team mounts a special substance called Intelligel. When Preston returns with new cushions for Ben's room, Ty decides they need

I pity the fool that messes with my design!

Ty and celebrity drop-in Mr. T duke it out to see who gets to control the bullhorn.

Sorry, Ty.

Things cool off quickly, however, when Ty tests the new backyard pool.

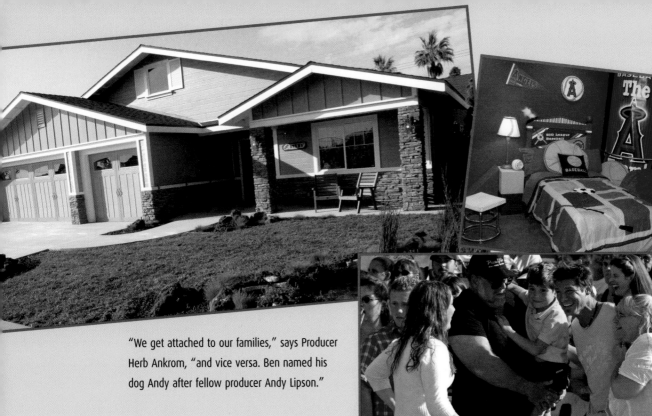

"We get attached to our families," says Producer Herb Ankrom, "and vice versa. Ben named his dog Andy after fellow producer Andy Lipson."

the celebrity test. He wants to be sure they are soft enough for Ben, so he enlists celebrity guest Mr. T to toss him into a pile of them. Mr. T is only too happy to take on the challenge! T-tested, the cushions are installed in the room.

With time to spare the renovation is nearly complete. The house looks fabulous. Of course, the real test is yet to come.

WELCOME TO YOUR **NEW HOME**

When the Burns see their new home, they are thrilled.

Jerry and Ellen admit it will be a huge relief knowing how much safer Ben will be.

But the rest of the family has not been forgotten. Pam, an inspiring fashion designer, is amazed that her room completely mirrors her interests and aspirations. With all the medical bills, her parents could not afford tuition for Pam at The Fashion Institute of Design and Merchandising. Now she won't have to worry about that: the Team has presented her with a scholarship!

For Jeff's room, Preston and Paul have come up with a music fan's dream: a guitar cabinet, a fret-board dresser, and a snare drum light fixture. Jeff is a cool California teen, into strumming his guitar and riding the waves on his surf-board. Ellen and Jerry needed space, and a new waterbed. The Team created a new master suite that exceeds their wildest dreams.

Diana, having given up so much to help out, needed a place of her own. Her new bedroom gives her that.

But Ben was the focus of the makeover, and his room was critical. The theme is simple. Ben loves baseball, so the Team enlisted the help of the Los Angeles Angels to create for Ben a bit of baseball heaven.

Ellen and Jerry, of course, are delighted that for once they can relax a bit knowing that their son is safe. And happy.

"Walking in the front door," Ellen says, "was like walking into paradise."

The family is so thankful for their good fortune. Especially dad Jerry. "I want Ben to be as normal a little boy as he can. Now he can."

Correa & Medeiros

FAMILIES

 "We didn't know how they were going to react to the idea of sharing a home," recalled Executive Producer Tom Forman. "We're all about building dream homes. This show was all about getting a family back on its feet, and having them move out as soon as possible."

Until recently, Frankie and Noreen Correa and their four kids—Alex, 14, Andrew, 11, Adam, 9, and 4-year-old Destiny—had been living a comfortable life. Frankie had a good job; they had a house. They were a happy family—until Frankie was laid off from his job. Unable to afford either the house or an apartment, the family shuttled from motel to motel. Finally, with no money left they were forced into an emergency homeless shelter, where they shared a tiny room and facilities with 20 families. Worse, since the shelter closes during the day, the family walks the streets of Denver, or rides city buses just to stay warm.

For Frankie, the situation is heartbreaking. "My kids got clothes on their backs. They got food in their stomachs," he says, tears welling in his eyes. "They're doing good, but to me, that's not good enough."

Dusty Medeiros is the mother of two boys, DaShawn, 8, and Deonte, 4. For eight years she has been working at a computer store. Then her life fell apart. The financial burden of raising her children and paying her rent became over-whelming, and she was forced to give up her home. Since then, Dusty and her kids have been staying on friends' couches.

Forman said the families liked the idea of sharing a home. "They said they knew what each had gone through. They had both been through tough times; this was their fresh start. They looked forward to it."

The Correa and Medeiros families have hit some rough times. They are making the best of awful situations. The good news is, things are finally about to change for the better.

Connie Zimmerman is founder and director of Colorado Homeless Families. Currently, her facility has space for 26 families, but there is not a bed to spare. What Zimmerman does have, however, is an empty lot.

She has appealed to the *Extreme Makeover: Home Edition* Team to help her create a new home so she can help more families who are in need.

THE HOUSE

The Correas are stunned when the Team arrives. They lead the Team on a tour of the facility, which is clean and functional, but that is about it. "It really changes your mind on what you think a homeless person is," says Ty.

Standing with her kids in front of her friend's house, meanwhile, Dusty Medeiros is overcome with emotion when the Team arrives. The two families meet, and realize soon they will be neighbors.

" Pack whatever you guys have...you will not be coming back to this shelter, ever. Once you leave here, you're coming with us." —Ty

WHEN THEMES COLLIDE

PAUL: AND THEN ON THIS SIDE, ON DUSTY'S SIDE, AND THE TWO BOYS, HAVE THE BEDROOM BE AN ARITHMETIC ROOM. UM...

PAUL: AN ARITHMETIC ROOM.

TEAM: IT SOUNDS BORING.

PAUL: OK. FINE.

TEAM: THIS CANNOT BE A BORING ROOM.

PAUL: NO. NO. ARITHMETIC. IT'LL BE GOOD.

THE RENOVATION STARTS NOW

The Design Team has one week, two families, and an empty lot.

The guiding principle will be function over form. The duplex will serve many families, and they want it to be around for a long time. It needs to be simple and sturdy!

Ty decides the Colorado Homeless Families center needs its own renovation.

By nightfall of Day 1, the builders are ready to pour the concrete. In Denver, where they have swelling soil, this is a bit tricky. Moisture can crack a standard foundation, so the foundation will be set on deep concrete pylons.

Landscape designer Eduardo plans to build a park for the entire community, including a playground and basketball court. He puts in a call to the Denver Nuggets. Star Kenyon Martin tells Paul and Eduardo to take whatever they need and even brings them back to the locker room to grab a few more things, including a pair of his sneakers.

By the end of Day 4, the house is finished. The Team wakes up on the morning of Day 6 to snow. Fortunately, the house—and the landscaping work—is just about done. By afternoon, the Team is able to move in the furniture. Meanwhile, Ty's renovation of the community center is behind schedule. He enlists the help of volunteers from Sears America Dream Campaign to finish the job. And by the morning of Day 7, the Team is ready to welcome back the families.

Paul DiMeo appears at a bit of a loss as a butterfly—or is he an angel? Meanwhile, his arithmetic bedroom has turned out to be anything but boring and the Medeiros kids love it.

WELCOME TO YOUR NEW HOME!

The Correa and Medeiros families erupt into laughter and tears when they see their new duplex.

Dusty Medeiros can't stop the tears as she walks through her new home. From the functional living room area and fully equipped kitchen to the arithmetic room for her kids, DaShawn and Deonte, she is almost speechless.

"I'm not one to do cartwheels. But if I could've, I probably would've."

Then she sees her own room, with its private bathroom. "I love the room. It was like something was lifted, because it was colorful and happy instead of being sad all the time."

Following the house tour, Ty leads both families out to see their brand new park, with a playground, basketball court, and picnic table. Eduardo has erected a sign with the name Renaissance Park, a suitable name to mark the rebirth of two families. Ty leads the entire Colorado Homeless Families community to their renovated community center. It features an entertainment center, desks and work tables, brand new computers, and a stunning wall mural of young Destiny's face.

Finally, Ty introduces the families to Mike Lennon from HomeAid and Steve Scarborough from Standard Pacific. Scarborough has the best gift of all for Frankie: a job at Standard Pacific.

Frankie feels blessed. "It's like God's given my wings back."

The whole tone of this show was different," said Executive Producer Tom Forman. "The idea was, if we had a chance to build a house for one homeless family, that's good. But if we could put a roof over a second family's head, that's even better. It's what this show is all about."

SOMETIMES,
YOU HAVE TO
DESTROY

BEFORE YOU CAN
CREATE.

Until recently, the Sears family enjoyed a normal life. Karen was a teacher's aide and single mom in Oakland, California. Jhyrve, 17, was in two choirs and loved watching movies with her friends. Lucas, 15, had dreams of being a pilot. Then, in February 2004, Jhyrve was diagnosed with Krabbe disease, a rare and potentially fatal genetic disorder that causes deterioration of nerve function. Suddenly their world changed. Karen quit her job and moved with Jhyrve to North Carolina for cutting-edge treatment at the Duke University Medical Center.

The treatment was successful, but it left Jhyrve's immune system severely weakened. Doctors insist that she cannot return to her home until the house is completely sterile. If she gets an infection, it could kill her. Unfortunately, the Sears' home has a severe mold infestation.

Paying both rent and a mortgage plus mounting medical bills means nothing is left for home repair. Meanwhile, back in Oakland, Lucas misses his mother and sister. Jhyrve misses her friends. Their situation was nearly hopeless.

"I just want to go home," wishes Jhyrve.

Back in Oakland, the Team is about to make that happen.

"We really need an environment for Jhyrve to go home to. If we don't make it, I don't know what I'm going to do. I don't know. I don't." —Karen Sears

THE HOUSE

"Good morning, Sears family! Karen, Jhyrve, and Luke! Wake up and come on out here!" The family is wide-eyed with joy when they see Ty. Unfortunately, Jhyrve is too ill to go on vacation. But Ty has news that makes her happy. "You're going home."

"We've got a week," he tells the Team. "Get a plan together. I'll get there as soon as I can."

The clear priority is making the home as clean and germ-free as humanly possible for Jhyrve, but without creating a gloomy "hospital feel."

The house is in okay shape except, at such a steep incline, water has been running onto it and creating a huge mold problem. Also, since Jhyrve needs a wheelchair until she regains strength, the hilly terrain around the house makes it very difficult to navigate.

THE RENOVATION STARTS NOW!

The severity of the mold problem convinces the Team the only option is to build a new home. The main theme will be to create as open and clean a living space as possible.

Day 2, and Ty arrives with contractors Lori and Dave Sanson. In a matter of minutes the house is rubble and the crew drags away the debris and prepares the site for framing. The walls are set in place, and the interior begins to take shape, including a large open area kitchen, sun room, and dining room on the first floor, and Jhyrve's and Karen's bedrooms on the second. Jhyrve has always wanted a bay window, so one is installed. Karen will have wonderful views of the hills near the home.

Some amazing technology is being put into place as well to ensure the house is as sterile as possible. Specially designed windows are installed that feature window treatments between the panes of glass to prevent excess dust build-up inside the home. Special moisture flashing goes up on the exterior

"Looking back..."

"...the right thing to do from a television production standpoint, was to wait to renovate until Jhyrve was stronger and healthier. It was really hard and very frightening for us to know that we needed to so thoroughly disinfect ourselves and our cameras and anything else that came into contact with her—or we could make her very, very sick.

It went slowly and it was difficult and very scary, but she really, really wanted to come home. This show was all about bringing Jhyrve home."

—Executive Producer Tom Forman

around all the windows. It will whisk moisture away so that nothing can get in to cause mold to grow in the walls. Mold-resistant sheetrock is also hung on the interior walls. Finally, a special electronic lift is installed to carry Jhyrve up the stairs until she is strong enough to climb on her own.

WELCOME TO YOUR NEW HOME!

Jhyrve's choir has joined the large crowd outside the home to serenade the Sears family with a special homecoming song. The song brings tears to their eyes. Then it is time to see their new home.

"Bus driver! Move that bus!"

It has been 10 months since Jhyrve has been home, and she is overcome. Inside the new home, Ty tells her she can take off her oxygen mask.

Karen is completely overwhelmed at her new kitchen, with its double-stack oven with a warming tray.

Lucas is thrilled with his flight-themed bedroom, especially with the Team's gift of 10 free round-trip airline tickets to anywhere Southwest Airlines flies. Perfect inspiration for a budding pilot!

When Jhyrve enters her room, she smiles like she's seldom smiled over the last many months. It has a jukebox, a neon sign, and a large projection television for watching her movies. She is thrilled.

For 10 months Karen Sears has put her life on hold for her daughter. Now it's her turn to relax. To help her do that, her new and very spacious bedroom features a stunning bathroom with a luxurious claw-foot tub.

Jhyrve's rehabilitation was foremost in Ty's mind when he took on his special project. He created an indoor fitness area where Jhyrve can continue her physiotherapy. It also features a continuous lapping pool, basically "a treadmill in water," that will help Jhyrve build up her strength.

Amazingly, the Sansons—their friends and employees—were so moved by Sears and the family's struggle that they collected $100,000 to help pay for Jhyrve's medical costs and to send both children to college.

Karen is moved almost beyond words: "You end up crying so much, there's almost no tears left. Thank you, I appreciate it very much."

Broadbent

FAMILY

A happy family portrait.
Patricia Broadbent poses with her greatest treasures, Trisha, Shaina, and Hydeia.

Patricia Broadbent's dedication to doing good makes people shake their heads in wonder. A longtime advocate of children's rights and a former social worker, she is mother to one child and has adopted six others. Three of the children, Hydeia, 20, Shaina, 16, and Trisha, 12, live at home. All three contracted AIDS from their birth mothers and are now living with the virus.

Following Hydeia's diagnosis as HIV positive in the 1980s, Patricia became a staunch advocate of AIDS awareness and acceptance. From the age of 6, Hydeia has joined her mother, rallying to bring understanding and assistance to people affected by HIV/AIDS. The two co-wrote a book, *You Get Past The Tears: A Memoir of Love and Survival*. Hydeia's current project is the STAR Program, which uses hip-hop music to raise consciousness about AIDS.

The AIDS virus ruins the body's immune system, making it difficult to fight off infections of all kinds. A simple cold could be fatal. Patricia worries that their run-down house in Las Vegas poses a health risk to her daughters, but she cannot afford the repairs to make the house germ-free and healthy.

More bad news followed when Patricia was diagnosed with cancer. She is in constant pain from the chemotherapy sessions, but refuses to complain. Her thoughts are only of what will happen to her daughters if she is gone.

"The house is just an object," she says. Her priorities are rock solid. "You can replace it. I can't get another Trisha and I can't get another Hydeia and I can't get another Shaina."

Patricia Broadbent needs peace of mind. The Extreme Makeover Team is on its way to do just that.

THE HOUSE

The Team has helped many deserving families, but they all agree that this family is special. They vow to do whatever it takes.

"Good morning, Broadbent family!"

It's an extremely emotional meeting between Patricia and the girls and the Team. Despite her own troubles and terrible pain, Patricia remains upbeat and optimistic. The Team is delighted to be able to deliver some very happy news. They are all headed to a fabulous getaway vacation to Jamaica. First, the Team needs a quick tour.

Immediately the Team spots signs of mold and bacteria, which can potentially be deadly for the girls. The kitchen doubles as a pharmacy for the huge amounts of refrigerated medication the girls require. The house is very small with tiny, cramped, and cluttered rooms, and shows familiar signs of fatigue, stress, and age. The backyard is nonlandscaped dirt, with an old swing set and a falling-down shed.

"The girls may not be able to stay together," worries Patricia at one point. "And I would just like to have some cohesiveness even if I'm not here."

The Team promises Patricia they will not let her or the girls down.

"I don't think of myself as dying of cancer. Any more than I think of the girls dying with AIDS. They live with AIDS."

—Patricia Broadbent

So unselfishly devoted to the needs of others, Patricia had no time—and no money—to take care of repairs. "This is one we really have to get right," Ty promises.

THE RENOVATION STARTS RIGHT NOW

The Team's priority is to create as germ-free an environment as possible. The second objective will be to create a beautiful and welcoming environment where Patricia and her daughters can feel safe and secure. The Team decides immediately to add lots of square footage to the house.

Each girl's room will be designed to suit her individual interests. Trisha is a musician; she's studying classical violin. For her the Team will create a bedroom based on a musical theme, including a small performance amphitheater, a beautiful viola nightstand, and her own cello. Hydeia loves to dance, but she's been too sick lately to "hit the clubs." So the Team decides to bring the club to her! Her room will be equipped with a unique LED pulsating dance floor and a disco ball. Shaina is into 1960s-era funk. She loves poetry and tie-dye, so the team will transform her room into a groovy Bohemian refuge with lava lamps and amazing magnetic walls where she can create poems with hundreds of stick-on words.

They come up with an inspired idea to locate small refrigerators in each room for medication. This will also help relieve the hospital sickroom feel of the kitchen and create a more joyous and warm area where the family can gather and share meals.

The game plan for Patricia is simple: over the top! This wonderful and incredible woman deserves only the absolute best. Ty has it covered. Her eye-popping new master suite will include a spacious private bathroom, huge hot tub, and working fireplace. Patricia likes to paint for relaxation and is a quite accomplished potter. As a bonus feature, the Team creates an arts-and-crafts loft, complete with three potters wheels, a kiln, and an easel.

The backyard will be redesigned and landscaped and will include a barbecue deck, an amazing in-ground pool featuring a rock grotto with a waterfall, and some gorgeous shrubbery, including guava vines, foxtail ferns, and magnolia trees. Lots of reminders of life and growth and continuity.

To kick off demolition Las Vegas-style, Ty invites famous boxing ring announcer Michael Buffer in what is billed as the "The Crumble in the Cul-de-Sac." It's a quick KO as the contractors knock the house down and out in no time. The contractor pours a new foundation and shortly a team of 150 framers begins raising the new skeleton. In an unbelievable eight hours the entire new two-storey house is up, walls and all!

Before closing off the ceilings, the contractors install a heavyweight filtration system from Switzerland that will scrub the air clean and keep the air fresh and bacteria-free.

With just hours to go before the family arrives home, the Team is ready to move the furniture into the home. Brand new furniture and appliances are set up in all the rooms, and the transformation of the house is complete.

Preston is nearly done landscaping the backyard. As an inspirational final touch, he plants a series of handmade bricks that bear single-word messages of hope.

"You pretty much make your own poem, make your own inspiration," he explains. "This seems like a perfect place to put them."

What happened to our designers?

"I'm Preston 'The Pugilist' Sharp and I'm joined by Paulie 'The Hammer' DiMeo in what can only be called the Crumble in the Cul-de-Sac."

WELCOME TO YOUR NEW HOME!

The turnout of friends and neighbors to welcome the Broadbents home is awe-inspiring. They carry signs and cheer wildly as Patricia and the girls climb from the limousine and stare wide-eyed and grin and wave. There are so many people that this woman has inspired with hope and courage.

But it's time to show them their new home!

"Driver! Move that bus!"

The Broadbents are overcome with emotion viewing their new home for the first time. The Team has captured each of their personalities perfectly. Ty leads the family to the garage, where the Team has parked a brand new Ford Freestyle adapted with hand controls so that Patricia can drive again. Even better, Bruce Karatz, the CEO of KB Home rips up Patricia's mortgage in front of her. No matter what happens, Patricia need never worry for the safety and welfare of her three beloved daughters.

"The 57 years I've been on this earth," recalls Patricia with humility, "I've had a lot of things done for me, but never in this magnitude."

Dore FAMILY

Roseanne Dore and her husband had a dream. They built a wonderful home together in the Pacific Northwest to raise their three daughters, Jessica, Sara, and Aariel. They planned to one day convert it into a bed and breakfast. Even when her husband died, Roseanne held on to that dream.

Then in March 2004, while the family was out for the evening, the house caught fire, and when they returned they were devastated to discover it had burned to the ground. There was nothing left. All their memories, their possessions, their dreams, had gone up in flames.

Not only was the insurance not enough to rebuild, but it was not even enough to haul the debris away. Homeless, Rosanne and her three daughters moved into a shed on the property. For nine months, they have been living with no electricity, no running water, and no bathroom, just an outhouse with no door. Meanwhile, the charred house was constant reminder of the family home that used to be.

Sadly, the improvised living situation was taking its toll on the family, causing the members to drift apart. The shed was so crowded and facilities so inadequate that the girls began sleeping over at friends' houses. The fire had destroyed more than a house, it had destroyed a family.

It needed to be put back together.

THE HOUSE

Because of the remote location, the Team trades in its bus for a ferryboat to get to a community on the Kitsap Peninsula, across the Puget Sound in northern Seattle. Once across the water, they travel on all-terrain vehicles through some of America's most beautiful countryside. But what they find at the end of the road is anything but beautiful. It's heartbreaking.

The fire damage is hard to conceive. But even more inconceivable is the idea that Roseanne and her three daughters have been living for so long in this tiny depressing shed.

"Good morning, Dore family!"

Needless to say, Roseanne and the girls are excited beyond belief that they have been selected for an extreme makeover. The Team realizes that it has arrived just in time. Ty sends the family off to a well-deserved vacation, and the Team sits down to map out a plan.

THE RENOVATION STARTS NOW

Preston pushes for a huge 3,000-square-foot house, a house the Team agrees will be spectacular enough to wipe out the terrible memories. They lay out an open-concept main floor with an enormous kitchen, large bright bedrooms for the girls, and a huge master suite for Rosanne.

The Team decides to design the girls' rooms to match their favorite activities. For Jessica, the oldest, that means a sailing room. For Sara, a skiing and snowboarding fanatic, the Team will put together a ski chalet room, complete with an authentic ski-lift chair. And for Aariel, a budding designer, it means an incredible designer room, including a large drafting desk and a 100-year-old working letterpress.

The house will also contain a fireplace that will be visible from anywhere on the main floor. It will serve as a symbolic statement from the Team that the family is secure from any more threat of fire. But just to be on the safe side, they incorporate state-of-the-art sprinkler systems throughout and a sophisticated alarm system in case of any fire emergency.

Inspired by the Dore's tragedy but impressed with spectacular natural and rugged beauty of the surroundings, Ty has decided to think BIG for his secret project. The Team is impressed—and, frankly, a bit worried.

There's a lot of work to do and the first thing is clearing away the charred wreckage of the old house. Ty finds some eager recruits to help with the demolition when he realizes there is a naval base in town. With the enthusiastic help of 165 Navy crewman and a team from HomeAid, the shed is torn down, the old house is removed, and the land is graded for its new foundation and framing. Watching the demolition via video link, Roseanne and the girls are only too happy to see the shed bulldozed into oblivion

Three hundred workers with prefabricated walls manage to complete framing for the huge new house in an astonishing 12 hours! The Team is literally blown away.

It has only been a few days but already the house is far along enough for the fine touches and decorating to begin. It's here that the Team has such an opportunity to give the Dore women the house they truly deserve. Preston comes up with a spectacular idea for huge spanning bookcases for the living room. He figures it will be an easy job for Ed, the new kid on the block and the the rookie on the Design Team.

Ed enthusiastically agrees, but after a torturous two days' straight laboring over the enormous project, Ed is exhausted and wondering what he has gotten himself into. Finally, the shelves are finished. Preston wanders by and seems impressed. "Great, now take 'em down!" Ed is flabbergasted, until he realizes he is being hazed.

Though the house will contain a wealth of new appliances and furniture, the Team is sensitive to the family's need for some mementos from their former world. Bricks salvaged from the old home are cleaned up and laid into the front step of the new house. Preston also salvages Roseanne's mother's table, a precious family treasure, and totally refurbishes it.

Meanwhile, Ty is still huddled inside his secret project. It comes together just in time for the Dores' arrival home.

WELCOME TO YOUR NEW HOME!

Some improvisation is necessary when the Team realizes that they will need something to replace the bus for the unveiling. What better symbol of the family's new home and the rebirth of a dream than a huge red fire engine!

With the fire engine in place, the limousine carrying the Dores pulls up in front of the house. "Move that...er...truck!"

Roseanne and the girls are more than thrilled with their new home. It's as big as a mansion. The Team has anticipated each of their needs perfectly. It is exactly as each had dreamed it might be. Now it's time for Ty to reveal his secret project.

Ty has built an entire bed-and-breakfast wing onto the house, which he has christened The Phoenix.

"It's the mythical bird that rises from the ashes. It's just kind of perfect if you think about it."

"I was overwhelmed," recalls Roseanne, "starting with the cheering of the crowd, everyone there in support of us. It was hard to believe our house could look so beautiful."

Adds Sara, "Wow. It was like Hollywood was here!"

WELCOME TO YOUR NEW HOME!

"What you didn't see on the air was the small city that had to be built just so we could get to the building site. We built roads, put up tents. We were serving thousands of meals a day. Everything had to be ferried in or brought in by helicopter. The contractor hired a firm whose other client was the US Army. How to feed a battalion on the move? That's the expertise they figured they needed to pull this off."

—Executive Producer
Tom Forman

FINAL THOUGHTS

"THIS IS SOMETHING THE GIRLS AND I HAVE DREAMED ABOUT. IT'S A DREAM COME TRUE."
—ROSEANNE DORE

Forman's Forum

THE POWERS EPISODE (FIRST EPISODE)

"I remember standing out on the street on reveal day thinking, 'What do we block the house with so the family doesn't see it? Do we use a big curtain...what? What about a bus?' And that seemed to work."

THE COX EPISODE

"This was the point in the season where the designers had gotten to know one another, and a lot of the newness had worn off. Everyone was tired, and they just... sort of...exploded. It was off camera and we aired some of it. We played it for laughs. Everyone was still pulling together, but the tension and stress was very real. It was a ton of work."

THE HARRIS EPISODE

"This is the first time we went into a neighborhood with police and sheriff's departments telling us this might not be a good place to shoot a television show. This was a neighborhood rocked by gang violence. But we were moved by the story, so we went in anyway."

THE ZITEK-GIL EPISODE

"What you didn't see on the show that nearly killed everyone was the family's driveway. It was like 70 degrees and probably 400 feet long. Every stick of lumber, every piece of furniture, every camera, every clipboard, every can of paint had to be hauled up by hand. It was brutal. And then it rained."

THE TUGWELL EPISODE

"We had been waiting for a marble countertop to come in from the Venetian Hotel in Las Vegas. A beautiful, beautiful, but very, very expensive marble countertop. Two had already been cracked in transit. So we were driving the family around the block, stalling them, while we unloaded the third. We were installing it as the family was coming into the bathroom for the reveal."

Executive Producer Tom Forman talks about what we didn't see...

THE POWELL EPISODE

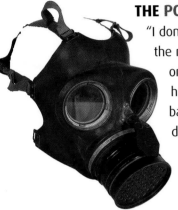

"I don't think they had any idea just how bad the mold problem was when they applied. It was only after we sent them off on vacation and had the mold tested that the results came back and we realized that these people could die! Not just Keenan, the whole family! The problem was that bad."

THE WALSWICK EPISODE

"This is the episode that Constance met her boyfriend J.J. And they were recently married! We actually have the tape where she and J.J. met. Who knew a year later they would be married?"

THE GRINNAN EPISODE

"Safety experts did all these calculations... on demolition and about where it would all fall. So we literally drew a line and said, 'If everybody is behind this line, we'll be okay.' Well, a slight miscalculation caused a wall to fall much closer to Ty than had been expected.

Ty ran. Our cameraman ran. It landed on our jib. The first jib-versus-house moment—but no way the last."

THE MACKEY EPISODE

"This was the episode where a huge shipment of bathroom fixtures and plumbing was inadvertently sent not to the Home Makeover set but to the cosmetic *Extreme Makeover* set. Learned about this on the second-to-last day. We sent Paige Hemmis in a pickup truck to get the stuff in the middle of the night."

THE GARAY EPISODE

"The first gang truce we ever negotiated. Before we felt it was safe to go in there, we sat down with the two local gangs and said, 'It just needs to stop. It needs to stop while we're here, and then it really needs to stay stopped.' And it was just so incredible to have these guys say, 'We get it. We will chill things out on that street. We promise.' And watch them—to this day—keep their word."

173

Episode List

Season 1

THE POWERS FAMILY
Their renovation plans took a back seat to fighting their daughter's leukemia. Now it's time!

THE WOSLUM FAMILY
With Dad called up to Iraq and Mom left to care for the three boys, there has been no time to care for this fixer-upper.

THE COX FAMILY
Down to the wire, the Team pulls off an all-nighter to give this music-loving family a new home and recording studio.

THE MENDOZA FAMILY
The Team adds square footage and a second storey for the first time—in the rain.

THE MCCRORY FAMILY
Expecting triplets, this family of five needs room to grow—and fast!

THE HARRIS FAMILY
A freak flood has caused structural damage to 'Sweet' Alice's home. She's spent her life helping others in Watts. Now it's payback time.

THE ZITEK-GIL FAMILY
Confined to a wheelchair after a car accident, this family's son is a prisoner in a house with too many stairs. Not for long!

THE HARDIN FAMILY
Cramped and badly outdated, the house is about to get the "Ponderosa" treatment.

THE TUGWELL FAMILY
The Tugwells, living in a hotel since a drunk driver crashed into their home, are about to get their life back.

THE WALSWICK FAMILY
Nine grieving kids and their recently widowed mother get the lift they need to start enjoying life again.

FRIENDS HELPING FRIENDS
The Team renovates a whole apartment in one day to say thanks to two September 11 New York City firefighter heroes.

THE POWELL FAMILY
Mold threatens the life of Carrie Powell's youngest son. The Team gives him a fresh start.

THE CADIGAN-SCOTT FAMILY
With both parents dying within weeks of each other, these eight youngsters need space and some fun in their lives.

THE IMBRIANI FAMILY
A "disaster waiting to happen," this home bites the dust as a tense Team wonders if it can build a new one in seven days.

Season 2

THE WOFFORD FAMILY
A huge, fully equipped gym will help this sports-loving family of nine recover from the loss of their mother.

THE GARAY FAMILY
After his mother was shot dead by a gang, Johhny added his five siblings to his own four children. They need more space!

THE POPE FAMILY
The Team's first and only night "door knock." The family's 12-year-old is poisoned by sunlight. This reno is a challenge.

THE GRINNAN FAMILY
Clean air and bacteria-resistant materials are the keys to making this home safe for a heart transplant recipient.

THE MACKEY FAMILY
Foster Mom Consuela needs space—accessible space for her wheelchair clients—so she can continue to serve her community.

THE ALI FAMILY
Lucy and her adopted sons lost their life savings to an unscrupulous contractor who destroyed their home. Help is on the way!

THE VARDON FAMILY
With deaf parents and a blind and autistic brother, teenager Stefan needs help to make the family's life easier.

THE ELCANO FAMILY

When her husband died in a car accident, Jennifer and her kids were barely able to keep their farm and home afloat. The Team fixes all that.

THE BURNS FAMILY

This family needs a safe environment for their youngest son who has brittle bones that break very easily.

THE BROADBENT FAMILY

Adoptive mother Patricia is fighting cancer and three of her daughters are living with AIDS. The Team goes over the top!

THE DORE FAMILY

Fire destroys the Dores' dream and the Team wants to get them out of the shed and into a real home again.

THE ANDERSON FAMILY

After being shot in a case of mistaken identity, son Rodney is left a quadriplegic. The small family home is not big enough to allow him even to use the bathroom.

THE SEARS FAMILY

Crippled by a rare nerve condition, 17-year-old Jhyrve needs a completely sterile home. Medical bills have eaten the family's savings—enter *EM:HE*.

THE MEDEIRAS/CORREA FAMILIES

Homeless through no fault of their own, these two families are about to share a brand new duplex.

THE HARPER FAMILY

Plumbing is the focus here—Ty has an appendectomy and runs the show from the hospital, while the Team tackles the sewage backup in this home.

THE HARRIS SEXTUPLETS

With a 9-year-old son and a miracle set of two-and-a-half-year-old sextuplets, this family needs more open space for their "circus."

THE OKVATH FAMILY

Eight-year-old Kassandra, the oldest of six has fought a two-year battle to recover from cancer treatment. Now she wants help to redecorate her hospital and her home.

THE LEOMITI-HIGGINS FAMILY

When the Higgins' parents die within months of each other, the Leomitis take in the children—with 11 in a small house they need help.

THE LESLIE FAMILY

The Leslies had reno plans for their 1870s home. But when her husband and oldest son died in an accident, Robin's focus turned to survival.

THE HARVEY FAMILY

Seven people share two bedrooms and one bath in this stark and decrepit home. Multiple hurricanes have damaged the exterior, too.

THE DOLAN FAMILY

The victim of a random shooting, James Dolan is now blind. He and his family need space and an easier environment for him to navigate.

THE JOHNSON FAMILY

Single dad Steven has five teens of his own and took in two more. As well as being a firefighter, he works two other jobs to keep the family going.

THE VITALE FAMILY

After losing his wife to leukemia, this police officer wants to give his three young boys the home their mother dreamed of.

THE PIESTAWA FAMILY

Five weeks into her term in Iraq, divorced mother of two Lori Piestawa becomes the first American woman killed in the war. Her parents and her children are in a mobile home, until the Team arrives.

That's a
wrap